JULIE STAFFORD'S

Juicing *for* Health

Modern production, processing, storing and cooking practices mean that on average we receive less than 50 per cent of the optimum nutrients required to maintain a healthy body.

'To counteract the effects of stress, the fast-food age and many of the pollutants that we are exposed to every day ... we will need far more vitamins, minerals and enzymes than are presently recommended. That means we will need to consume more fruit and vegetables than even the most disciplined of us do now. **The best way to obtain the benefits of large amounts of produce is to drink fresh juice.**'

Julie Stafford is the highly acclaimed author of the bestselling *Taste of Life* cookbooks, which have sold more than 1.5 million copies worldwide. When her husband, Bruce, was diagnosed as having cancer, Julie became vitally interested in the relationship between diet and disease. She modified her favourite recipes and invented new ones that were low in fat and cholesterol, had no added sugar or salt, were high in fibre, and tasted delicious. Publication of her first *Taste of Life* cookbook followed Bruce's remarkable remission.

JULIE STAFFORD'S

Juicing
for
Health

Over 200 recipes for fruit & vegetable juices, soups, smoothies & sorbets

TUTTLE PUBLISHING
Tokyo • Rutland, Vermont • Singapore

This book could not have been completed without the help of my wonderful assistant, Vicki O'Keefe. I would also like to thank everyone at the Eastwood Fruit Supply Shop, Ballarat, who take great pride in their fresh fruit and vegetables.

First United States publication 1994

Published by Charles E. Tuttle Co., Inc.
364 Innovation Drive
North Clarendon, VT 05759-9436
Tel: (802) 773-8930
Fax: (802) 773-6993
Email: info@tuttlepublishing.com
Web site: www.tuttlepublishing.com

ISBN 0-8048-3040-1

Library of Congress Catalog Card Number: 94060892

First published by Penguin Books Australia Ltd 1994

Penguin Books Australia Ltd
250 Camberwell Road
Camberwell, Victoria 3124, Australia

Cover design by Beth McKinlay
Design by Meredith Parslow
Photography by Alan Lindsay
Food styling by Helen Clucas
Typeset in 11/13 Times by Bookset, Melbourne, Australia

Printed in China through Bookbuilders

TUTTLE PUBLISHING ® is a registered trademark of Tuttle Publishing.

Contents

Introduction

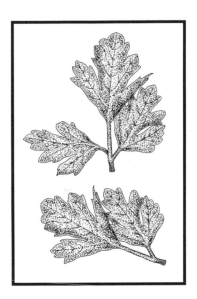

In order for the human body to function efficiently it needs a regular supply of high-quality nutrients in the right combination and concentration. The interaction of these nutrients is the basis of good health and wellbeing.

The best way of obtaining these nutrients is through eating fresh fruit and vegetables: human beings are living things and we need a large proportion of our food intake to be living also. Fruit and vegetables, especially in their raw state, contain living enzymes that are essential in the breaking down and absorption of nutrients.

Fruit and vegetables may also provide the key components of disease-beating agents. We already know that the cruciferous vegetable and onion families can stimulate the production of certain types of cancer-fighting enzymes. Broccoli, for example, contains the chemical sulforaphane, which triggers enzymes that break down cancer-causing chemicals and allow them to be flushed from the body. The high fluid content of fruit and vegetables assists this flushing of wastes and toxins, while also providing valuable nutrients.

In the last decade health organisations have stressed the importance of eating more fresh fruit and vegetables. Most suggest that we eat 5–9 servings daily. That can be as much as 1.5 kg (3½ lbs) of produce!

It may not, in fact, be enough to eat more fruit and vegetables. To maximise the value of the nutrients and enzymes for the promotion of good health and prevention of disease, and to counteract the effects of stress, the fast-food age and many of the environmental pollutants that we are exposed to every day, it is not unrealistic to assume that in time we will need far *more* vitamins, minerals and enzymes than are presently recommended. That means we will need to consume more fruit and vegetables than even the most disciplined of us do now.

The solution is, in fact, simple. The best way to obtain the benefits of large amounts of produce is to drink fresh juice. And the best juice to drink is that extracted by a juicer – unhindered by fibre, which requires digestion, all the goodness in the juice goes straight into the bloodstream for instant effect.

This book is not about justifying the need for more fruit and vegetables in our diet. It accepts without doubt the valuable contribution that fruit and vegetables play in the prevention of disease, promotion of good health and as potential disease beaters. I certainly recommend that fruit and vegetables are eaten in their whole, raw state. However, and more importantly, I highly recommend that fresh juices are consumed in order to complement, enhance and increase the amount of nutrients and food enzymes in our diet.

By using *Juicing for Health* you will learn the health benefits of each juice and how simple it is to prepare flavoursome, thirst-quenching and nutritious drinks. You will be amazed, as I have been, at how quickly you will experience the benefits of fresh juices. By adding two or three juices to an already well-balanced diet you will notice a change in just days! An investment in a juicer has to be one of the best investments in good health today.

Juicing – the New Health Revolution

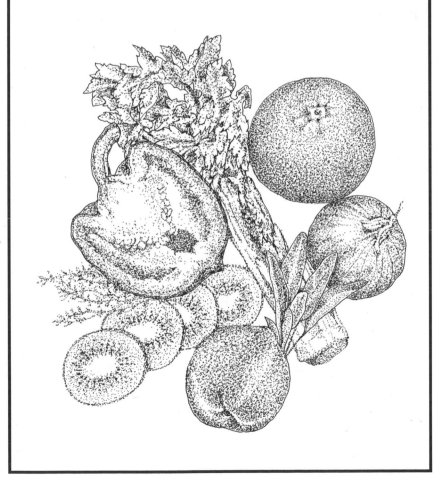

Fresh Juice – the Secret of Good Health

In the 1980s our eating habits were challenged and changed forever when a health and nutrition revolution, with its emphasis on low-fat, low-cholesterol, sugar-free, salt-free and high-fibre foods, took place. Now we are about to witness an extension of that revolution through the use of fresh and natural juice. The addition of fresh juices to a well-balanced diet *immediately* makes eating habits healthier.

- Juices are full of nutrients and enzymes that help fight diseases and promote a healthy and strong immune system.

- Juices provide instant nutrition. Because they are fibre-free they are rapidly absorbed and go to work immediately – healing, energising, revitalising and generating healthy growth.

- Juices provide instant sustainable energy that can increase performance potential, unlike the 'quick-fix' energy that is associated with high-fat, high-sugar junk foods.

- Juices are filling while being low in kilojoules and high in water, and they also speed up the body's metabolism.

- Juices can assist in alleviating stress by correcting the body's acid/alkaline balance.

- Juices can play an important part in anti-cancer and cancer-healing diets.

The Therapeutic Nature of Juices

The human body needs at least 8–10 glasses of fluid each day. Most people take this fluid in the form of coffee, tea and alcohol. These are all acid-forming, which can be detrimental to our health and the way we feel, and also contain stimulants that are addictive by nature. They tend to dehydrate rather than add vital fluids to the body. Alcohol is fattening and caffeine in coffee and tea unrealistically raises our blood-sugar levels. In addition, tap water today varies greatly in its composition.

On the other hand fresh fruit and vegetable juices are high in vitamins, minerals and enzymes. They are also alkaline in nature, which in itself is therapeutic.

Juices are easily digested and assimilated, allowing maximum nutrient value to be absorbed at a faster rate without the body expending unnecessary energy. Toxins and wastes are easily and efficiently eliminated from the body.

By following a purely fresh fruit and vegetable juice diet for short periods or by adding fresh juices to an already well-balanced diet, you can help accelerate and enhance the process of restoring chemically starved body tissues. In this way you will not only restore the body to good health, but possibly defer the ageing process, prevent poor health and the onset of many of our so-called modern-day degenerative diseases.

Many experts today believe that it is the enzymes found in raw foods that hold the key to our wellbeing and longevity. These enzymes are not only responsible for breaking down elements within foods to make them more digestible and nutritionally valuable, but they are also known to stimulate certain types of cancer-fighting enzymes. These 'phase two' enzymes break down cancer-causing chemicals such as car fumes or nitrites, which are present in cured, pickled and highly salted foods, and allow the body to flush them from the system before they cause cellular damage to tissue. These enzymes are destroyed when we heat and cook food.

By adding fresh juices to your diet you will automatically improve your health. Just on a day-to-day basis you will look and feel better as your skin, hair, eyes and nails begin to show the benefits of drinking fresh juice. You will also be pleasantly surprised at your new-found energy and the need for much less sleep as your body flushes toxic material from its system and replaces it with the life-giving forces of juices, which also heighten your mental awareness and ability to taste foods more definitively. Best of all, though, juices taste delicious!

The potassium/sodium factor

In the early 1920s a young German physician, Dr Max Gerson, first raised the theory that the beginning of all chronic illness lies in the potassium/sodium imbalance in the body. Potassium is an important nerve conductor and acts as a catalyst for many body enzymes. It is an important alkalising agent and maintains the acid/alkaline balance in the blood and tissues. Potassium is essential for muscle contraction and proper heart function and the liver uses it in the production of glycogen from glucose (liver glycogen regulates the level of sugar in the blood; in muscles, glycogen is converted to glucose when the body needs energy). It promotes the secretion of hormones and helps the kidneys to detoxify blood. Too little potassium can cause high blood-pressure and can lead to chronic fatigue.

Sodium is closely linked to potassium and chlorine in carrying out many vital functions in the body. They work together to neutralise acids and maintain electrolyte balance – the fatigue-combatting ability of certain essential minerals – in cells. They also regulate body fluid levels.

Sodium and potassium are nutritional antagonists. We need to have them in balance for good health. Our diet today tends to have an over-abundance of sodium – we add salt when cooking, during the processing of foods and at the table. Many drugs also contain high levels of sodium. This excess sodium leaches vital potassium from cells, disturbing their vital function, thereby creating an environment for disease.

Gerson believed that by correcting this imbalance by eating potassium-rich foods the body would be invigorated and cleansed as respiration was improved at the cellular level. Potassium-rich food, he believed, would also mobilise white blood cells, which fight and destroy cancer cells. Using this theory, Gerson cured his own chronic migraines, when specialists had failed, by experimenting with diet until his condition improved. Through these experiments he developed a diet of fresh fruit and vegetables, which he also used successfully to treat other migraine sufferers as well as a patient with lupus (a tuberculosis of the skin), at a time when there was no known cure for lupus. However, it was not until Gerson cured Albert Schweitzer's wife of a severe case of tuberculosis of the lung that he fully realised the importance of his fresh fruit and vegetable diet.

The symptoms of cellular breakdown begin with fatigue and decreased immunity and end in disease. Raw foods rich in potassium (see 'Minerals in Fruit and Vegetables', page 41) bring about cellular recharge and the potential for an environment that stimulates good health. A diet high in fresh juices is one way of correcting the potassium/sodium imbalance and achieving the level of health that is our birthright.

The acid/alkaline factor and stress

The acid/alkaline balance in the body is central to good health. An acid environment results in a lack of energy, chronic fatigue and susceptibility to disease. If you are stressed your acid/alkaline balance is out of kilter – emotional stress can be the result of a chemical imbalance of ingredients that, in the proper proportions, can otherwise help you 'ride the storm'.

However, stress can come in many forms. A diet based on acid-forming ingredients, such as coffee, sugar, meat, white flour and processed foods, will also make you feel stressed (some of us do not recognise this state as we have never experienced an unstressed state). Hormones released by the body in a stressed state are also acid-forming.

As all fruit and vegetables are highly alkaline, drinking fresh juice is the easiest way to correct an acid/alkaline imbalance. Fig juice and all green juices are particularly alkaline-forming. Watch your intake of acid-forming foods, such as oysters, fish, meat, eggs, rice and nuts, if you are prone to an acid/alkaline imbalance (note that while grains tend to be acid-forming, sprouted seeds and grains become alkaline in the sprouting process).

Chlorophyll

Chlorophyll, found in all leafy green vegetables (especially kale, alfalfa, cabbage, spinach, lettuce, watercress, wheatgrass, parsley, celery, cucumber and green capsicum), is recognised as a powerful blood and cell builder, internal body cleanser and potent regenerative tonic. The chlorophyll molecule is similar to that of haemoglobin, which carries oxygen from the lungs to the tissues.

Chlorophyll has been used in the past to treat heart disease, athero-sclerosis (a form of hardened arteries), sinusitis, osteomyelitis and depression with impressive results. It is also believed to be capable of blocking the genetic changes brought about by cancer-causing substances.

Amino acids

There are eight major amino acids that the body can only synthesise from fresh foods: lysine, leucine, tryptophan, phenylalanine, threonine, valine, methionine and isoleucine, all of which are essential for the maintenance of health. If these amino acids are not present in the diet the body is unable to rejuvenate cells properly. A deficiency of just one of these amino acids can cause ill health and premature ageing, while children need them all for growth and good health.

All fresh juices contain amino acids that are easily digested, the high-est concentration being found in sprouts and leafy green vegetables.

Enzymes

Many would argue that food enzymes are just another protein and use-ful amino acids from which new proteins are built by the body. How-ever, there is another argument that suggests these food enzymes are essential for the body to break down and fully utilise the nutrients in our foods. When we heat foods we destroy these enzymes, making it difficult for the enzymes in our gut to digest them further. As a result the nutritional value can be lost.

Enzymes found in raw food are believed to be a powerful support mechanism for the body's own enzyme system. Foods in their raw state contain vitamins, minerals and trace elements, along with the right enzymes to help break down the food. When food minus its natural enzymes is eaten unnecessary stress is placed on the body's ability to produce these enzymes.

Bioflavonoids

Bioflavonoids, pigments found in concentrated levels in the pith of most citrus fruit and in lesser amounts in all raw plant food, are known to have a potent health-enhancing and restorative effect. Two of the vital ingredients of bioflavonoids – nobiletin and tangeretin – assist certain enzymes to rid the body of drugs, heavy metals and car-exhaust fumes, which are associated with causing the cellular damage that becomes the environment for cancer. So, indirectly these bioflavonoids play a role in cancer prevention. Remember, when you juice citrus fruits, always leave a little of the white pith on.

Fresh Juices vs. Bottled Juices

Fresh juice is undoubtedly the superior choice over bottled juice when it comes to nutritional value and taste. Commercial varieties go through many processes before they reach the supermarket shelves. In order to prolong shelf life these juices are pasteurised by being heated to very high temperatures. This process kills the living enzymes as well as the sensitive vitamin C. Manufacturers make up for this by adding a synthetic vitamin C to the juice (see below). Manufacturers also often add artificial colours and flavours, sugar, corn syrup, salt and chemicals that further destroy the nutrients in the original juice and that can be harmful to our health. As the juice is exposed to uneven temperatures and light in the warehouse and supermarket it continues to lose more nutrients.

So-called 'natural' juices are often made by boiling down fruit juice to make a concentrate that is reconstituted with water. This juice (now deficient of enzymes) can only be as good as the water that is used to reconstitute it. Some of these concentrates are made from fruit and vegetables imported from countries that use chemicals and carcinogenic pesticides that may have been banned in this country.

By drinking freshly juiced fruit and vegetables you are assured of the purest, most potent and correctly proportioned form of nutrition available.

Synthetic vs. Natural Vitamins and Minerals

Many people are under the assumption that they can correct nutritionally deficient diets by supplementing them with synthetically produced vitamins and minerals. They can't. Synthetic vitamins and minerals are manufactured from chemicals and 'dead foods'. These synthetic vitamins and minerals are not absorbed efficiently, if at all, because they lack the living enzymes essential to carry out this process. Living enzymes are *only* found in fresh raw foods.

Many forms of supplements only provide one or two nutrients. In this form these nutrients are not digested or absorbed because they need a proportion of other nutrients to make this possible. This difficulty is not encountered when using fruit and vegetable juices to add a specific nutrient to your diet.

Researchers are still defining the nutrients found in fresh fruit and vegetables and new nutrients, such as alpha-carotene, phenols, indoles, aromatic isothiocyanates, terpenes and organo-sulphur compounds, continue to be identified. It is more than likely that without these elements in our foods we may not be able to get the maximum benefit from other nutrients. Their absence may even be detrimental to our health. As yet most synthetic supplements do not contain these elements.

One way to effectively supply our bodies with the most natural vitamins and minerals possible is to consume a wide variety of organically grown and naturally ripened fresh foods.

Fibre-free Juices

While juices made by using a juice extractor are high in nutrition they are low in fibre. Most juicers will extract the juice from the fibre in the juicing process. Some of the better juicers go as far as spin-drying the fruit and vegetable fibre to extract as much liquid as possible, resulting in a very clear, fine juice. The juice extracted in this latter stage holds the richest source of nutrients.

Digestion is a slow process. Foods have to be chewed in order to activate enzymes, which in turn begin a chemical process that starts to break down the foods and unlocks their nutrients. Because the juice machine has extracted the juice from the fibrous part of the fruit or vegetable it has already begun the 'digestion process' for us. Uninhibited by fibre, which would otherwise need to be broken down and digested, the carbohydrates, vitamins, minerals and enzymes in fresh juice go directly into the bloodstream for immediate effect. (Patients who are unable to digest 'heavy foods' – high-protein, high-fat, highly processed foods – and who lose their appetite due to illness can benefit especially through the intake of fibre-free juices.)

It is not my intention to encourage you to substitute fresh fruit and vegetable juices for the real, whole thing. However, by adding juices to a diet that already includes a variety of fresh fruit and vegetables, high-fibre cereals, grains and legumes you can increase the potency of your nutrient intake and help prevent and fight disease.

You can, of course, use the extracted fruit and vegetable fibre to obtain maximum health benefits. Flavour soups with the reserved fibre or thicken casseroles with it. You can also increase the fibre content of cakes, muffins and scones by using the extracted pulp, which provides wonderful flavour and moisture as well.

Equipment and Produce

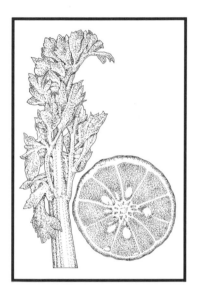

The juicers required to produce fibre-free juice, which I am recommending here, are known as juice extractors and can be used for both fruit and vegetables. When juicing citrus fruit, however, a citrus juicer will give the best results.

Before purchasing a juicer it is important to weigh up your needs and fully understand the options available. Once you have made your selection the next step is to choose the best fruit and vegetables possible and learn how to store them so that they retain a high level of nutrients.

Juice Extractors

Although juice extractors may vary in size and appearance they all work by the same principle. Fruit and vegetables are fed by means of a safety plunger down a tube onto a rotating fine blade. The blade extracts the juice while retaining the fibre in a process similar to that of spin-dry cycle on a washing machine, which removes water from clothes by centrifugal force.

There are many fruit and vegetable juice extractors on the market; all of which cater for different needs. To choose the one that's right for you, consider the following.

- Look at the capacity and size of the juicer. Will the machine make the quantity of juice required by your family easily and efficiently?
- Is the juicer a good-looking machine? Will you be happy to leave it out on your kitchen bench or will it look cumbersome and out of place? (This may not seem important at the time of purchase but if you pack your juicer away after each use it will soon become 'out of sight out of mind'.)
- Is the juicer easy to dismantle, clean and re-assemble? Check that the parts are all sturdy. Beware machines that have many small parts, which invariably get lost and are often irreplaceable.
- Some machines include an anti-froth baffle that gives a very clear, fine juice. The froth contains nutrients, however, and adds a creamy texture to your juice when stirred through, so whether you wish to retain or exclude it becomes a matter of personal choice.

Cleaning your juicer
To clean the juicer simply unlock the safety catches and empty out the retained fibre. A small brush is useful when cleaning the blade. Should the plastic components of the juicer become discolored wipe them with a soft cloth that has been dipped in a little vegetable oil, or soak the parts overnight in a white vinegar solution. Do *not* place the motor unit in water to clean it. Simply wipe it over with a damp cloth.

Citrus Juicers

There are many kinds of citrus juicers available, from manually operated ones to electrically driven models. Citrus juicers differ from juice extractors in that they squeeze the juice from the fruit rather than extract it by centrifugal force. This means the juice still contains much of its fibre. Of course, it is also possible to make citrus juice using a juice extractor.

Fresh is Best – Organic is Better!

When buying fruit or vegetables for juicing always choose fresh (ideally just-picked), firm, unblemished, in-season produce. The fresher the produce the better: an hour after having been picked these foods start to lose their vital nutrients. (With this in mind it is a great idea to grow your own. You don't need a large plot, however. Many fruit and vegetable plants can be grown very successfully in pots on balconies.)

Another option is to buy organically grown produce, which is becoming more readily available at markets, supermarkets, greengrocers and from 'pick-your-own' farms. (As before, choose the freshest fruit and vegetables possible.) We add juices to our diets in an attempt to provide good nutrition and optimal health, so it stands to reason that we should look for the very healthiest produce to juice. Although it may be a little more expensive, consider organic produce as an investment in good health. If we keep asking for organically grown foods we will eventually eliminate the need for producers to use artificial and potentially harmful pesticides and fertilisers. At the same time we will be testing their skills to come up with healthier ways of maintaining crop production.

Buy small amounts of fruit and vegetables at a time to ensure freshness. Store the produce in the refrigerator in plastic bags or the vegetable crisper. When packing the produce for storage don't discard the outer leaves of vegetables such as lettuce or cabbage or the tops of celery. It is here that the blood-purifying vitamin C is mostly found. Also, don't leave prepared fruit and vegetables to soak in water as the food value is leached out. This is especially true for vitamin C, which is also destroyed when heating and storing foods for a long time.

Before you juice, simply wash the produce to remove any dirt, insects and residual sprays. A small scrubbing brush is ideal for moving stubborn dirt. It is best to leave the skin on fruit such as apples, apricots, peaches and pears and vegetables such as carrots, parsnips and beetroot as the most valuable nutrients are often found just below the skin's surface. A mild solution of pure castile soap (available at health food stores) will remove most pesticide residues below the skin's surface.

Getting the Most Out of Your Juice

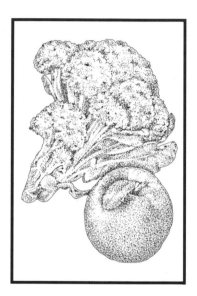

Fresh juices are potent drinks that need to be treated with some care. If your aim is to top up your diet with extra nutrients by drinking juices you need to know how and when to drink them and the side effects you may experience.

How to Drink Fresh Juices

It is best to drink fresh fruit or vegetable juices on an empty stomach and between meals, or to substitute a meal with a juice. Fresh fruit and vegetable juices break down more quickly than whole foods so if you combine juices with whole foods the concentrated sugars and starches in juices can ferment in the digestive tract while waiting for the whole foods to be broken down. If you are having a fresh juice as part of a meal, allow half an hour after drinking the juice before eating.

Juices should be drunk immediately they are prepared. Vitamins and minerals are lost when juice is stored for any length of time. In addition, once the juice comes in contact with air it begins to oxidise and putrefy.

Fresh fruit and vegetable juices are very potent drinks. Some may need diluting with natural spring water or other juices (beetroot or green juice, for example), while *all* juices should be sipped slowly. Many juice experts suggest that juice should be 'chewed' before swallowing. This allows the enzymes in the juices to mix with the enzymes in saliva to begin the digestion and assimilation process.

When to Drink Fresh Juices

Juices can be drunk any time during the day! Try them before or in between meals or replace a meal with juice.

Breakfast
Why not start your day with a delicious, refreshing and energy-packed juice? Taken first thing in the morning fresh juice helps to eliminate food residue from the night, and sometimes the day before. It cleanses the stomach and digestive tract and allows the body to absorb fully the nutrients of foods that follow. If you plan to have cereal as well, allow half an hour after drinking the juice before eating.

Morning break
Stay clear of snacks loaded with refined sugar and empty calories! The natural sugar in juices will keep your energy levels up and feed the brain the food it needs to perform. Don't forget tea and coffee tend to dehydrate the body. If you need to cut back on your sugar intake, try a vegetable juice, which has half the kilojoules of fruit juice.

Lunch
Complement a well-balanced lunch with a tasty juice. Allow half an hour after drinking juice before eating to obtain maximum effects.

Afternoon tea
As the body starts to wind down and begins to tire a fresh juice will keep your energy levels up, provide extra nutrients and top up the fluids needed to carry out bodily functions.

Pre-dinner drink
Alcohol, like tea and coffee, dehydrates the body of essential fluids. Try some of the vegetable juices as a pre-dinner cocktail instead.

Nightcap
Some juices have a relaxing effect on the nervous system. Allow at least two hours after eating food before drinking a juice nightcap.

Too Much of a Good Thing?

There is no evidence to suggest that you can drink too much juice. On the contrary, the more juice you drink the quicker the processes of restoration, rejuvenation and detoxification will occur. At least 500 ml/ 16 fl oz/2 cups of juice should be consumed daily in order to enhance nutrition and precipitate the preventative and restorative qualities of juices. Anything from 1–4 litres/1¾–7 pints/1–4¼ quarts can be consumed for optimal health benefits. The Gerson cancer diet, for example, recommends drinking 10–12 glasses of fresh juice daily, including carrot, apple and green juice. To try and eat the amount of nutrients found in this amount of juice in one day would be impossible. It takes 4 kg/ 9 lbs of carrots to make ten glasses of carrot juice!

Some carrot juice devotees have noticed that their skin becomes a yellow–orange colour after drinking a lot of juice. It was thought this indicated too much carrot juice. But we now know that the change in skin colour is a sign that the kidneys are working overtime to eliminate the poisonous wastes and the bladder, unable to cope with the volume of fluid, directs the elimination process to the pores of the skin, which is another perfectly healthy method of ridding the body of toxins. If this occurs you should continue to drink the juices and help the process of elimination by drinking lots of spring water and herbal teas.

Combining Juices

I know of no scientific explanation that suggests combining fruit and vegetable juices is harmful. However, there are juice experts who argue that some fruit and vegetables should never be mixed. They believe that combining juices produces possible related symptoms, such as stomach and intestinal gas, stomach and abdominal pains, indigestion and even allergies. Not all people are affected in the same way, however. It is probably best to let your taste buds be the judge and to work out your own preferred combinations. If you do not experience any of the above or other symptoms within two hours of consuming the juice then you should not have a problem.

Juicing Tips

- Juice only the freshest fruit and vegetables and choose organically grown produce whenever possible.
- Drink your juices immediately they are juiced to get the maximum nutritional benefits and taste. Juices begin to break down when exposed to air and lose many of their vital properties.
- Stir the juice before drinking to incorporate the froth for a creamier consistency. Remember that the froth is full of goodness too.
- Juices are best drunk on an empty stomach.
- Potent juices, such as beetroot and green juices, should be drunk in small amounts and preferably diluted with water or other juices.
- Vegetable juices contain approximately half the kilojoule value of fruit juices so drink them freely.
- Many herbs are rich in vitamins, minerals and chlorophyll. Add some

to your favourite vegetable juices for extra nutrition and to vary the flavour.

- Limit fruit juices to reduce kilojoule consumption or if you have any health disorders related to sugar intake, for example diabetes or hypoglycaemia.
- Don't discard the fruit fibre. Add water to it and boil it down to make a syrup water for flavouring sorbets or cooking fruits (see page 163).
- Fibre from strawberries, blueberries, raspberries and blackberries can be added to plain low-fat yoghurt or to home-made ice-cream. It can also be added to cakes and muffins for colour, flavour and extra moisture.
- Vegetable fibre can be added to soups and casseroles. Store your vegetable fibre in the refrigerator and use it to make soup stock. Just add water, some garlic or ginger, diced onion and water. Simmer for at least an hour, strain and use for soup stock, making gravy or for thinning pasta sauces or white sauces.
- Carrot fibre is excellent added to breads, scones or muffins before cooking. It will add a wonderful orange colour, extra fibre and moisture.
- Remember to leave on half the white pith of citrus fruit as the pith contains valuable bioflavonoids (see pages 9 and 39).
- The pips in citrus fruit and the seeds of capsicums can add a bitter flavour to your juices, so it is best to remove them before juicing.
- Soft fruits, such as banana and avocado, are best puréed to make juices and soups rather than pushed through a juicing machine.
- Wash your machine thoroughly each time you use it as some juices will stain machines and leave a sour taste.

Juicing for Health

Drinking juices regularly will greatly improve your general health and wellbeing. Even more benefits can be enjoyed if juices are used to cleanse and eliminate toxins, and they can play a helpful role in slimming diets too. With even greater implications are the very real benefits that fresh fruit and vegetable juices can provide as part of an anti-cancer diet.

Cleansing Diets

The reason for using juices as a cleansing or elimination therapy will vary from person to person but most often the results will be the same – a much improved state of wellbeing.

A doctor will often examine your tongue to determine your internal state of health. When the tongue has a white or yellowish coating it usually indicates that all is not well. This is a most opportune time to begin an internal cleanse using juices to remove poison and bring about a correct balance in the intestinal flora by establishing an environment for healing. However, you do not have to wait until you feel unwell to undergo a cleansing or elimination procedure. It is probably wise for everyone to drink only juices for several days at least once or twice a year as a preventative measure for many illnesses.

When you replace lower-quality foods with higher-quality foods such as fruit and vegetables you may experience some symptoms of change. (Some people, however, do not experience any side effects at all.) The essential enzymes, amino acids, minerals, vitamins, trace elements and carbohydrates in fresh fruit and vegetables create a 'life force' that is capable of reproducing healthy tissue. Any changes experienced, there-fore, should be seen as having a positive effect and will be temporary. The human body always tries to produce good health. The self-curing nature of many conditions, such as colds and cuts, shows how the body tends towards good health unless our interference is too great.

The symptoms of change you may experience when beginning to drink juice in any quantity may include headaches, fever and/or colds, your skin may break out and you may experience weakness, nervous-ness or trembling, irritability, negativity or depression, frequent urina-tion, and nausea and/or vomiting. Bowel motions should become softer and be of a lighter colour. Sometimes diarrhoea occurs but this is usu-ally only temporary. The intestinal flora changes as all putrefied foods and any toxic build-up are eliminated from the bowel and the colon membranes are cleansed and revitalised. Harmful bacteria are replaced by healthy bacteria that diminish intestinal gas, reduce inflammation of the intestinal tract and correct bowel action. The symptoms will vary according to the materials being discarded, the condition of the organs involved and the energy needed during the cleansing and elimination process. As the poisons are eliminated any symptoms will disappear.

It is important to understand the cleansing and elimination process and not confuse the sometimes unpleasant symptoms for illness. You should avoid taking drugs or massive doses of vitamins to alleviate these symptoms. Instead, you should continue to flush your system by drinking as much fluid as possible (in between your nutritional juices drink plenty of water – at least 8–10 glasses daily).

Should you experience any major discomfort consult your medical practitioner immediately to discuss the nature of your cleansing diet.

Slimming Diets

Being overweight predisposes you to a lower quality of life and makes you more susceptible to disease. The more fat you carry, the more stress is placed on your immune and cardiovascular systems. If you are overweight you will have a higher proportion of fat in your blood, which tends to make it acidic. The more acidic the blood, the more susceptible you are to related illnesses. Fresh fruit and vegetables, especially in their raw state, have a counteractive alkalinising effect and, as such, should form a part of *any* diet but should feature especially in a weight-loss programme. By building a slimming diet around juices, lots of fresh fruit and vegetables, low-fat and high-fibre foods you will be surprised how easily and quickly you can lose weight.

Most slimming diets are potentially starvation diets – starvation of kilojoules and important vitamins and minerals. The low-kilojoule and high-nutrient value of fresh vegetable and fruit juices, however, make them an ideal meal substitute or snack for anyone on a slimming programme. A 250 ml/8 fl oz glass of vegetable juice contains about 250 kilojoules/60 calories, while the same amount of fruit juice is about 500 kilojoules/120 calories.

Carrot, spinach, beetroot and cucumber juices are highly recommended for use in a weight-loss programme. Carrot juice is not only one of the most delicious vegetable juices but it is also one of the most versatile as it complements and combines well with most other juices. It is high in nutrients such as vitamins B, C, D, E, K and beta-carotene and stimulates the adrenal glands, which encourage fat to be burned.

To lose weight you need to reduce your kilojoule intake while also increasing the number of kilojoules used daily by doing more exercise. There are five simple steps to follow when using fresh juices as part of a weight-loss programme.

1 Drink 6–8 glasses of fresh juice each day. Only two of these should be fruit juice, which is higher in kilojoules than vegetable juice.
2 Eat small meals of pasta, rice, salads and vegetables in between drinking the juices.
3 Substitute fish for red meat.
4 Eat plenty of wholegrain bread.
5 Choose low-fat dairy products, such as yoghurt.

One of the traps people fall into when slimming is to skip breakfast.

This starts the day off badly and leads to lethargy, irritability and mid-morning hunger pangs. Cravings for a 'quick fix', usually snacks and fast foods loaded with hidden fat and sugar, then set in. These cravings are a sign of malnutrition. If a diet is devoid of essential vitamins and minerals, the body demands more and more kilojoules in an attempt to find some sort of nutritional balance. This is an appetite that can never be satisfied: it is not hungry for food but for nutrients. We can eliminate this malnutrition by eating nutrient-rich foods regularly. By including a variety of fresh juices in a well-balanced diet these cravings are immediately curbed because the body is satisfied.

It takes little time to prepare a healthy, satisfying, low-kilojoule fresh juice. Just one glass of juice for breakfast, for example, is sustaining and leaves the stomach feeling full. Because juice is low in kilojoules breakfast could also consist of low-fat yoghurt and berries, muesli with low-fat milk or wholemeal toast with a sugar-free spread.

Next time you feel like a quick snack compare the approximate kilojoule value of the following snack foods with that of a glass of fresh vegetable juice.

	quantity	kilojoules	calories
fresh vegetable juice	**250 ml/8 fl oz/1 cup**	**252**	**60**
Coca-cola	250 ml/8 fl oz/1 cup	455	120
dried apricots	50 g/2 oz	555	132
peanuts	50 g/2 oz	712	170
sweet cream biscuits (2)		780	186
lemon cordial	80 ml/3 fl oz/⅓ cup	839	200
cheese (50 g) and biscuit		839	200
chocolate-coated vanilla ice-cream	100 g/3½ oz	1062	253
potato chips (fried)	100 g/3½ oz	1150	274
hot dog		1205	287
jam doughnut		1323	315
chocolate cake with icing	100 g/3½ oz	1550	369
fruit cake	100 g/3½ oz	1596	380
chocolate milkshake	250 ml/8 fl oz/1 cup	1768	421
chocolate bar (plain)	100 g/3½ oz	2236	532
potato crisps	100 g/3½ oz	2270	540
pistachio nuts (shelled)	100 g/3½ oz	2487	592

Anti-cancer Diets

Fresh natural juice, which is full of vitamins, minerals, trace elements, natural sugars, proteins and live enzymes, is a vital ingredient in an anti-cancer diet. Fibre-free juice provides nutrition in a concentrated form that can be absorbed effortlessly into the bloodstream, where it goes to work immediately, protecting against disease and creating an environment for healing to occur.

In most cases of chronic disease lowered cell respiration is obvious. This is especially true in many cancers. The director of the Max Planck Institute for Cell Physiology in Berlin, biochemist Otto Warburg, discovered in the early 1930s that cancer cells derive their energy from a glucose-based chemistry whereas healthy cells derive their energy from oxygen-based chemistry. Cancer and other degenerative diseases (such as heart disease, diabetes, arthritis, asthma and allergies) appear to be the development of cellular respiration in trauma. The symptoms are fatigue, a lowering of immunity and, finally, disease.

A raw-food diet, especially using juices, has the ability to correct cell respiration and in doing so increases the body's immunity to disease. Most prudent cancer diets today encourage a generous intake of foods rich in vitamin C and carotene (a substance found mainly in fruit and vegetables that the body converts to vitamin A). People who consume generous amounts of foods containing these vitamins have a lower risk of developing cancer. Laboratory studies on animals and cancer cells suggest that carotene suppresses cancer and that vitamin C may prevent the formation of nitrosamines, which are carcinogenic substances. Taking synthetic vitamin A in high doses is not recommended as it becomes toxic when in the body. Large doses of vitamin A derived from carotene does not, however, appear to produce the same toxins.

Studies also show the populations that eat substantial amounts of the cruciferous vegetables (cabbage, cauliflower, broccoli and Brussels sprouts) have a lower incidence of cancer of the large bowel. Sprouted seeds and grains are also beneficial in an anti-cancer diet as when they are broken down in the body they release two chemicals – cyanide and benzaldehyde. Normal body cells are able to protect themselves against these chemicals but cancer cells are incapable of doing so and as a result these chemicals become powerful cancer-fighting agents. By juicing these vegetables you can obtain even more of their vital ingredients and live enzymes. Add their wonderful fibre to soups and casseroles for extra flavour and goodness.

Anti-cancer diets also promote a reduction in the amount of fats we eat. High-fat diets are linked to several types of cancer, including bowel and breast cancer. By substituting juices, fresh fruit and vegetables and high-fibre foods for high-fat meals we not only eliminate fat from our diet but we eliminate a major risk factor for developing cancer and other diseases.

Juicing-based raw-food diets eliminate wastes and toxic material that have accumulated in the body tissue and organs. Juices also restore the vital potassium/sodium balance (see page 7) and break down acids and promote an alkaline environment, which is essential for good health (see page 8).

Fresh fruit and vegetable juices supply more than enough essential nutrients for healthy cells, allowing them more oxygen take-up to produce the energy required for normal cell function and protection from disease.

Vitamins, Minerals and RDIs

In the 1980s the National Health and Medical Research Council of Australia revised its tables that recommend daily intakes of specific nutrients (see pages 29 and 30). In these tables it can be seen that the recommended daily intake (RDI) varies from individual to individual, depending on the sex, age and health of a particular person and, if female, whether she is pregnant or lactating.

In recent times, however, the acceptance of RDIs has begun to be questioned. We now recognise that there are wide variations in the needs for nutrients: each of us can no longer be measured as an 'average' individual. One thing that has remained constant, it must be recognised, is that the further a person's intake of nutrients falls *below* the

RECOMMENDED DIETARY INTAKES OF VITAMINS PER DAY

GROUP	AGE	VITAMIN A μg retinol equivalents	VITAMIN B1 mg	VITAMIN B2 mg	VITAMIN B3 mg niacin equivalents	VITAMIN B6 mg	TOTAL FOLATE μg	VITAMIN B12 μg	VITAMIN C mg	VITAMIN E mg alphatocopherol equivalent
Infants	0–6 mth									
	Breastfed	425	0	0	4	0"	50	0	25	2
	Bottlefed	425	0	0	4	0"	50	0	25	4
	7–12 mth	300	0	0	7	0β	75	0	30	4
Children (male and female)	1–3 yr	300	0	0	9–10	0–0	100	1	30	5
	4–7 yr	350	0	1	11–13	0–1	100	1	30	6
Boys	8–11 yr	500	0	1	14–16	1–1	150	1	30	8
	12–15 yr	725	1	1	19–21	1–2	200	2	30	10
	16–18 yr	750	1	1	20–22	1–2	200	2	40	11
Girls	8–11 yr	500	0	1	14–16	1–1	150	1	30	8
	12–15 yr	725	1	1	17–19	1–1	200	2	30	9
	16–18 yr	750	0	1	15–17	1–1	200	2	30	8
Men	19–64 yr	750	1	1	18–20	1–1	200	2	40	10
	64 + yr	750	0	1	14–17	1–1	200	2	40	10
Women	19–54 yr	750	0	1	12–14	0–1	200	2	30	7
	54 + yr	750	0	1	10–12	0–1	200	2	30	7
Pregnant		750	1	1	14–16	1–1	400	3	60	7
Lactating		1200	1	1	17–19	1–2	350	2	60	9

These figures were revised between 1982 and 1987. Note that mg = 1 thousand of a gram, and μg = 1 millionth of a gram. The table is supplied by the National Health and Medical Research Council of Australia.

RECOMMENDED DIETARY INTAKES OF MINERALS PER DAY

SUBJECT	AGE	CALCIUM mg	IRON mg	MAGNESIUM mg	ZINC mg	IODINE µg	SODIUM mmol	SODIUM mg	POTASSIUM mmol	POTASSIUM mg	SELENIUM µg	PHOSPHORUS mg
Infants	0–6 mth Breastfed	300	0	40	3–6	60	6–12	(140–280)	10–15	(390–580)	10	150
	Formula fed	300	3									
	7–12 mth	550	9	60	4–6	60	14–25	(320–580)	12–35	(470–1370)	15	300
Children (male and female)	1–3 yr	700	6–8	80	4–6	70	14–50	(320–1150)	25–70	(980–2730)	25	500
	4–7 yr	800	6–8	110	6–9	90	20–75	(460–1730)	40–100	(1560–3900)	30	700
Boys	8–11 yr	800	6–8	180	9–14	120	26–100	(600–2300)	50–140	(1950–5460)	50	800
	12–15 yr	1200	10–13	260	12–18	150	40–100	(920–2300)	50–140	(1950–5460)	85	1200
	16–18 yr	1000	10–13	320	12–18	150	40–100	(920–2300)	50–140	(1950–5460)	85	1100
Girls	8–11 yr	900	6–8	160	9–14	120	26–100	(600–2300)	50–140	(1950–5460)	50	800
	12–15 yr	1000	10–13	240	12–18	120	40–100	(920–2300)	50–140	(1950–5460)	70	1200
	16–18 yr	800	10–13	270	12–18	120	40–100	(920–2300)	50–140	(1950–5460)	70	1100
Men	19–64 yr	800	5–7	320	12–16	150	40–100	(920–2300)	50–140	(1950–5460)	85	1000
	65 + yr	800	5–7	320	12–16	150	40–100	(920–2300)	50–140	(1950–5460)	85	1000
Women	19–54 yr	800	12–16	270	12–16	120	40–100	(920–2300)	50–140	(1950–5460)	70	1000
	55 + yr	1000	7	270	12–16	120	40–100	(920–2300)	50–140	(1950–5460)	70	1000
Pregnant		+ 300	22–36	+ 30	16–21	+ 30	40–100	(920–2300)	50–140	(1950–5460)	+ 10	+ 200
Lactating		+ 400	12–16	+ 70	18–22	+ 50	40–100	(920–2300)	65–140	(2540–5460)	+ 15	+ 200

These figures were revised between 1982 and 1987. Pregnant women should note that the necessary iron intake is not achievable from dietary iron; all pregnant women should thus receive supplementary iron. The table is supplied by the National Health and Medical Research Council of Australia. A millimole (mmol) is a scientific measurement representing weight in milligrams divided by the equivalent weight.

suggested RDIs given in the NHMRCA tables, the greater the likelihood that his or her diet is deficient. As a result, susceptibility to disease is increased as the immune system is weakened. Using the tables this way is certainly helpful.

Nutrition is constantly being redefined. Today's challenge is to improve the quality as well as the length of life and we are now moving away from diets that focus on the macronutritional (proteins, carbohydrates and fats) to foods with high micronutritional (vitamin and mineral) values. These foods provide maximum health benefits and maintain optimal function.

Fruit and vegetables, as you will see in the nutrients tables featured in the juice recipes (see pages 51–149), come packaged with a variety of vitamins and minerals. These elements are in balance with each other, offering the body one of the best possible sources of essential ingredients. These vitamins and minerals are also accompanied by enzymes, which increase the potential of the body to absorb nutrients efficiently.

In the past we were guided more often than not by RDIs when looking for deficiencies in diet. Today we accept the importance of following a well-balanced diet that is high in vitamins and minerals and low in fats. Eating lots of fruit and vegetables and drinking plenty of fresh juice will ensure you enjoy all the health benefits available to you.

Vitamins in Fruit and Vegetables

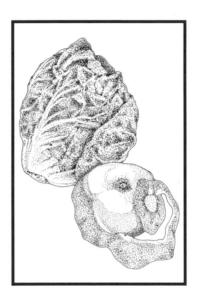

Vitamins are chemical compounds needed in regular small amounts for the body to function. They regulate the chemical reactions by which the body converts food into energy and living tissue. Without vitamins we become susceptible to disease. Use the following vitamin profiles in conjunction with the recipes for juices, smoothies, soups and sorbets for maximum nutritional benefit. You will find profiles of essential minerals on pages 41–46.

Vitamin A

Vitamin A occurs naturally only in animals. However, some plants contain substances called 'carotenes' or 'provitamins A', which the body converts to vitamin A.

Vitamin A is essential for the development of the growing foetus. It also helps maintain the skin, eyes, urinary tract and lining of the nervous, respiratory and digestive systems. It is especially necessary for the growth of bones and healthy teeth. Beta-carotene is a known anti-oxidant that helps prevent and heal certain forms of cancer.

Common sources suitable for juicing
The fruit and vegetables that provide carotenes include apricots and melons and green or yellow vegetables, especially alfalfa, broccoli, capsicum, carrot, cress, parsley, spinach and turnip greens.

Health benefits
Vitamin A increases the body's resistance to infection of the urinary and respiratory tracts, maintains skin in a moist condition and keeps it free from dermatosis, is essential for proper growth and vision, increases resistance to colds, promotes and maintains good digestion and appetite and is essential for lactation and reproduction.

Signs of deficiency
A lack of vitamin A can result in dry, scaly skin; retarded growth; poor bone and teeth development; lack of stamina; diarrhoea; sinus troubles; catarrh; ear abscesses; night blindness; loss of appetite and poor digestion; formation of gall and kidney stones; sterility; respiratory infections and lowered resistance to skin infections.

Vitamin B1

Vitamin B1 (thiamine) is necessary for the metabolism of fats and carbohydrates and it helps the heart and nervous system to function properly. Vitamin B1 is not stored by the body for any length of time so needs to be consumed regularly.

Common sources suitable for juicing
Minute amounts of vitamin B1 are found in most fresh fruit and vegetables.

Health benefits
Vitamin B1 aids appetite, absorption of foods and digestion; promotes growth; increases resistance to infection; is essential for nerve tissues to function properly; is required to increase the weight and accelerate

the growth of children; influences intestinal mobility; plays a role in carbohydrate metabolism; is essential for lactation; aids liver function and improves muscle tone.

Signs of deficiency
A lack of vitamin B1 can result in poor appetite, slow heartbeat, general weakness, nervousness, intestinal and gastric disorders, poor lactation, erosions and ulcers of the stomach, hypertrophy of adrenals and pancreas, beriberi, depression, constipation, irritability and sciatica.

Vitamin B2

Vitamin B2 (riboflavin) is essential for cell respiration. It also promotes tissue repair and healthy skin.

Common sources suitable for juicing
Capsicum, mushrooms and all leafy green vegetables are high in vitamin B2 and are suitable to juice.

Health benefits
Vitamin B2 increases resistance to disease; delays degeneration; improves skin and eye conditions; aids liver, kidney and heart function; is essential for the healthy function of the gastro-intestinal tract; helps the body assimilate iron and aids protein metabolism.

Signs of deficiency
A lack of vitamin B2 can result in cracked lips; lip and tongue inflammation; burning, itching eyes; cataracts; photophobia; blurred vision; retarded growth; digestive disturbances; loss of hair; loss of weight; pellagra; vaginal itching; oily skin and hair and birth deformities.

Vitamin B3

Vitamin B3 (niacin) is a co-enzyme in fat synthesis and is essential to hydrogen transportation. It also helps to maintain healthy skin.

Common sources suitable for juicing
Minute amounts of vitamin B3 are found in most fruit and vegetables, especially sprouts and citrus fruit.

Health benefits
Vitamin B3 builds mental health, aids the nervous system, maintains appetite and aids the adrenal glands.

Signs of deficiency
A lack of vitamin B3 can result in pellagra, gastro-intestinal troubles, skin and neurological changes, irritability, bad breath, ulcers and insomnia.

Vitamin B5

Vitamin B5 (pantothenic acid) stimulates the adrenal glands and is associated with the production of adrenal hormones as well as the development and growth of the central nervous system. It is said to protect against damage caused by excessive radiation, and is an essential co-enzyme in carbohydrate, fat and protein metabolism.

Common sources suitable for juicing
Vitamin B5 is found in all green vegetables, especially sprouts, and citrus fruit.

Health benefits
Vitamin B5 aids the production of adrenal hormones, is central to the development and growth of the nervous system, promotes natural antibodies, maintains healthy skin and hair and aids liver function.

Signs of deficiency
A lack of vitamin B5 can result in psychosomatic disorders, low blood sugar, low blood pressure, cramps, insomnia, allergies, asthma, loss of appetite, nausea, abdominal pain, repeated infections, fainting sensations, disturbed electrolyte and water balance and stress.

Vitamin B6

Vitamin B6 (pyridoxine) is essential in some thirty enzyme reactions, the metabolism of protein and lipids, the synthesis of the non-essential amino acids and in the production of hormones and bile. It is essential for healthy teeth, gums, blood vessels, nervous system and red blood cells.

Common sources suitable for juicing
The fruit most suitable for juicing that are high in vitamin B6 are oranges, lemons and bananas. All vegetables, but especially cabbage, provide vitamin B6.

Health benefits
Vitamin B6 is essential for the nervous system; promotes good appetite; maintains healthy teeth, gums, blood vessels, and red blood cells; aids liver function and is beneficial to pregnant women.

Signs of deficiency
A lack of vitamin B6 can result in depression, sleepiness, loss of appetite, nausea, seborrhoeic dermatosis, sore lips and tongue, conjunctivitis, pains in the arms and legs, hypochromic anaemia, convulsions, premenstrual oedema, muscular weakness and infections.

Vitamin B9

Vitamin B9 (folic acid) is a co-enzyme to B12 and is consequently essential in the formation of red blood cells. It is also important in the production of antibodies.

Common sources suitable for juicing
The vegetables most suitable for juicing that are high in vitamin B9 include all leafy green vegetables, beans and mushrooms.

Health benefits
Vitamin B9 aids the gastro-intestinal tract and helps build healthy blood.

Signs of deficiency
A lack of vitamin B9 can result in megablastic anaemia, diarrhoea, menstrual problems, dropsy and malabsorption syndromes.

Vitamin B12

Vitamin B12 (cyanocobalamin) is essential for the development of red blood cells and assists in the proper function of the nervous system.

Common sources suitable for juicing
Mushrooms are high in vitamin B12 and can be juiced successfully.

Health benefits
Vitamin B12 is necessary for the growth and formation of blood cells and body tissue, promotes nerve cell regeneration and is recommended for vegetarians.

Signs of deficiency
A lack of vitamin B12 can result in anaemia, dermatosis and neuritis.

Vitamin B13

Vitamin B13 (orotic acid) is essential in the synthesis of the nucleic acids and is vital to the regenerative process. Some therapists regard it as a specific remedy in the treatment of multiple sclerosis.

Common sources suitable for juicing
All root vegetables are high in vitamin B13 and can be juiced successfully.

Health benefits
Vitamin B13 promotes the excretion of uric acid, aids the development of heart muscle and assists in the assimilation of minerals into the cell.

Signs of deficiency
Any severe systemic degeneration may result from a gross lack of vitamin B13, although this has not been proved.

Choline

Choline is another of the B-complex vitamins. It is essential for proper fat metabolism, in which it seems to work with inositol and lecithin and vitamins A, D, E and K, and minimises deposits of fat and cholesterol. Choline is also necessary for the synthesis of the nucleic acids and is one of the important members of the B-complex associated with the formation of the myelin sheathing of nerves.

Common sources suitable for juicing
All leafy green vegetables are high in choline and can be juiced successfully.

Health benefits
Choline helps in the maintenance of healthy arteries.

Signs of deficiency
A lack of choline can result in raised blood pressure, cirrhosis, fatty degeneration of the liver, atherosclerosis, muscle weakness and degeneration of the kidneys, adrenals, lungs, eyes and heart.

Inositol

Another B-complex vitamin, inositol is a fat dissolver and partner to choline. It is one of the active ingredients in lecithin and an important factor in the health of the heart muscles and brain-cell nutrition.

Common sources suitable for juicing
Citrus fruit and green vegetables are high in inositol and can be juiced.

Health benefits
Inositol maintains healthy hair, delays hardening of the arteries and promotes growth and cell survival in bone marrow, eye membranes and intestines.

Signs of deficiency
A lack of inositol can result in loss of hair, retarded growth, reproduction failure, dermatitis, constipation and high blood-cholesterol levels.

Vitamin C

Vitamin C (ascorbic acid) is used in healing as an anti-inflammatory and to treat allergies, infections and shock. It is essential for sound bones and teeth.

Common sources suitable for juicing
Acerola berries, citrus fruit, rosehips, tomatoes, capsicum, chillies, parsley and all green vegetables, especially broccoli and cabbage, are high in vitamin C and can be juiced successfully.

Health benefits
Vitamin C promotes bone and tooth formation and growth, improves appetite, raises resistance to infection and bacterial toxins, keeps blood

vessels in a healthy condition, protects the heart, distributes and diffuses calcium to tissues from the blood and is necessary for normal adrenal function.

Signs of deficiency
A lack of vitamin C can result in physical weakness, a shortness of breath, rapid heart action and respiration, tendency to disease of the heart and blood vessels, restlessness, impaired digestion, headaches, defective teeth, swollen spongy gums, poor lactation, tender joints, broken bones that won't knit, bone abscesses, a decrease in resistance to infection, peptic and duodenal ulcers, secondary anaemia, a reduction of haemoglobin, impaired adrenal function, scurvy, bruising and a sallow complexion.

Bioflavonoids

Bioflavonoids are a complex of vitamins known variously as vitamin P, citrin, hesperidin and rutin – all of which are considered part of the vitamin C complex. They have a strengthening effect in the capillary walls, and act as an anticoagulant and antihistamine. Bioflavonoids also prevent the destruction of vitamin C in the body by oxidation, and are beneficial in a supporting role in all the conditions for which vitamin C is a specific remedy.

Common sources suitable for juicing
The pith of grapefruit, oranges, tangerines and lemons is high in bioflavonoids, as are blackcurrants, and all these fruit can be juiced successfully.

Health benefits
Bioflavonoids maintain the walls of small blood vessels; help combat oedema, dropsy, diabetes and diseases of the joints; assist in arresting haemorrhages; aid the treatment of high-blood pressure and cataracts; fight infectious bacteria, viruses and fungi, and assist in ridding the body of drugs, heavy metals and car-exhaust fumes (therefore they could also be seen as preventing the cellular changes that bring about cancer).

Signs of deficiency
A lack of bioflavonoids can result in capillary fragility and ensuing conditions, oedema and bruising.

Vitamin E

Vitamin E (tocopherols) has been known as the heart and geriatric vitamin because of its anti-oxidant properties. It helps prevent the oxidation of polyunsaturated fatty acids in cell membranes and other body structures.

Common sources suitable for juicing
Leafy green vegetables, leeks, cabbage, Brussels sprouts, herbs and sprouts are all high in vitamin E and can be juiced successfully.

Health benefits
Vitamin E is essential for growth after sexual maturity, has been known to counteract sterility, strengthens the heart, appears to have some function in regulating the pituitary gland, stimulates the thyroid gland, promotes vigour, stimulates metabolism, is a known anticoagulant, maintains skin cells and body membranes and heals burns.

Signs of deficiency
A lack of vitamin E can result in sterility, muscle degeneration, miscarriage and deficient lactation.

Vitamin K

Vitamin K (menadione) is essential for the production of prothrombin, a co-enzyme in the blood-clotting process.

Common sources suitable for juicing
All green vegetables suitable for juicing, especially lettuce, cabbage, cauliflower, spinach and alfalfa sprouts, are high in vitamin K.

Health benefits
Vitamin K assists in blood-clotting and in the neonatal period is used to treat and prevent haemorrhagic diseases of babies.

Signs of deficiency
A lack of vitamin K can result in lowered vitality, nosebleed, miscarriage, cellular disease and diarrhoea.

Minerals in Fruit and Vegetables

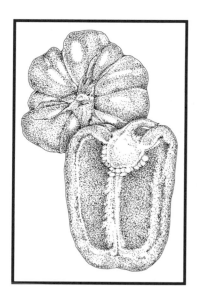

Minerals are required by the body to ensure growth and the maintenance of structure and composition of digestive juices and fluids that are found in and around cells. Calcium and phosphorus, for example, are needed in comparatively large amounts for the formation of healthy bones and, along with magnesium, are essential for the development of good, strong teeth. Calcium is also needed to assist blood-clotting. Some minerals are only required in small amounts, such as iron, which is an important component of haemoglobin, the oxygen-carrying substance present in red blood cells. While other minerals, including copper, zinc, manganese and potassium, are only needed in the body in very small quantities, they all play vital roles in the chemical processes that result in the release of energy or synthesis of protein.

Use the following mineral profiles in conjunction with the recipes for juices, smoothies, soups and sorbets for maximum nutritional benefit. You will find profiles of essential vitamins on pages 32–40.

Calcium

Calcium is usually associated with bone development and maintenance but it actually plays a role in the construction of all tissues. It assists in normal blood-clotting, muscle action, nerve and heart function and maintains the acid/alkaline balance of the blood.

Common sources suitable for juicing
Green leafy vegetables, especially kale and including endive and cabbage, are high in calcium, as are carrots and blackberries.

Health benefits
Calcium assists in the formation of bones and teeth, blood-clotting, maintaining heart rhythm, nerve tranquilisation and transmission, muscle growth and contraction and the permeability of cell membranes.

Signs of deficiency
A lack of calcium can result in heart palpitations, insomnia, muscle cramps, nervous disorders, tooth decay, osteoporosis, brittle fingernails and rickets.

Cobalt

Cobalt helps maintain red blood cells and activates a number of enzymes in the body. It also functions as part of vitamin B12.

Common sources suitable for jucing
All ripe fruit and green vegetables contain cobalt.

Health benefits
Cobalt facilitates the function of haemoglobin.

Signs of deficiency
A lack of cobalt can result in anaemia.

Copper

Although copper is present in small amounts in the body's tissues, especially the spleen and liver, and in red blood cells, it still needs to be taken in through diet to ensure normal red blood cell formation.

Common sources suitable for juicing
All green vegetables suitable for juicing contain copper.

Health benefits
Copper helps in the formation of red blood cells and enzymes. It also works with vitamin C to produce elastin, which is central to healthy cartilage, ligaments and artery walls and facilitates bone formation, hair and skin colour, the healing and mental process and helps maintain a balanced mental state.

Signs of deficiency
A lack of copper results in weakness, sores that don't heal, diarrhoea in infants and anaemia.

Iron

Iron phosphate is essential for the formation of haemoglobin and myoglobin in the blood. It is also important in the healing of injuries to the soft tissues and where inflammation and fevers are present and helps break down protein and promotes growth.

Common sources suitable for juicing
Asparagus, lettuce, spinach and apricots are all rich in iron.

Health benefits
Iron helps haemoglobin production, promotes growth in children and increases resistance to stress and disease.

Signs of deficiency
A lack of iron can result in breathing difficulties, brittle fingernails, anaemia, fatigue, constipation and a sore or inflamed tongue.

Magnesium

Magnesium is the main constituent of white nerve fibres. It acts as a catalyst in the utilisation of carbohydrates, fat, protein, calcium, phosphorus and potassium.

Common sources suitable for juicing
All dark green vegetables contain magnesium.

Health benefits
Magnesium aids the body's acid/alkaline balance and the metabolism of vitamin C and calcium. It also leads to increased energy levels and speeds up the body's metabolism.

Signs of deficiency
A lack of magnesium can lead to confusion, mood swings, a rapid pulse, tremors and nervousness.

Manganese

Manganese is an essential activator of enzymes and is necessary for normal skeletal development and functioning of the brain and the maintenance of sex hormones.

Common sources suitable for juicing
Manganese is found in apples, apricots, pineapples and all green leafy vegetables.

Health benefits
Manganese facilitates enzyme activation, the utilisation of vitamin E, sex hormone production and the metabolism of vitamin B1, fat and carbohydrate.

Signs of deficiency
A lack of manganese can result in dizziness, ringing in the ears, hearing loss and a slow metabolism.

Phosphorus

Phosphorus is found in bones, teeth, blood, hair, nerve tissue and the brain.

Common sources suitable for juicing
Any type of bean suitable for juicing is high in phosphorus.

Health benefits
Phosphorus aids the development of bones and teeth, cell formation and repair, energy production, heart-muscle contraction, kidney function, the metabolism of calcium and sugar, vitamin utilisation and nerve and muscle activity.

Signs of deficiency
A lack of phosphorus can result in fatigue, no appetite, difficulty in breathing, obesity and weight loss.

Potassium

Potassium is responsible for the electrochemical balance of tissues of the heart and all other muscles and is the main healing element in the body.

Common sources suitable for juicing
Avocados, beans, corn, endive, garlic, kale, leeks, mushrooms, parsley, parsnips, silverbeet and spinach are all high in potassium.

Health benefits
Potassium aids regular heart beat, rapid growth, muscle contraction, nerve tranquilisation and kidney function.

Signs of deficiency
A lack of potassium can result in acne, continuous thirst, dry skin, constipation, general muscle weakness, muscle damage, insomnia, nervousness, slow irregular heartbeat and weak reflexes.

Silicon

Silicon is a constituent of bone, tissue, organ and nerve sheath, hair, nails and skin.

Common sources suitable for juicing
Strawberries are a wonderful source of silicon.

Health benefits
Silicon helps bone calcification, conditions the skin and ensures a healthy thyroid gland.

Signs of deficiency
A lack of silicon can result in bone decalcification, tendonitis and cardiovascular disease.

Sodium

Sodium is the key element in the body and is an important aid in the digestion of food and the viscosity of the blood. It also keeps calcium in solution so that it can reach all the body's tissues. Sodium controls the distribution of water in the body to stimulate the liver and pancreas. Along with potassium, calcium and magnesium, sodium works to neutralise the acids in the body.

Common sources suitable for juicing
Asparagus, beans, celery, kale, parsley, silverbeet, spinach and turnips are all high in sodium.

Health benefits
Sodium keeps cellular fluid to its normal level, aids proper muscle contraction and maintains the blood and lymph system.

Signs of deficiency
A lack of sodium can result in loss of appetite, intestinal gas, muscle shrinkage, vomiting and weight loss.

The Recipes

Fruit Juices

The recipes in this section are intended only as a guideline – let your imagination run wild and titillate your taste buds by creating your own recipes! That's the fun thing about juicing – just by adding a little more apple or pear, a few strawberries or perhaps your favourite spice you can dramatically change the end result and discover delicious and energising combinations. As you experiment don't forget to record your successful juice combinations so that you can enjoy them again.

Remember: fruit juices are high in natural sugar. Therefore, if you want to reduce your kilojoule intake or you have health problems related to high sugar levels you should limit the amount of fruit juice you drink and balance it with plenty of vegetable juice. To reduce the amount of natural sugar I suggest you dilute the juice with water or cucumber juice, which is suitable because it tastes bland. I have included a sug-gested dilution ratio at the end of the first recipe for each fruit. Adjust the ratio to suit your personal taste or health needs.

The first recipe listed for each fruit also indicates the quantity of that particular fruit needed to make up a cup (250 ml/8 fl oz) of that juice. When you first begin drinking fresh juice you may find this amount too much. Start with a quarter or half the quantity (diluting it if desired) and slowly increase the amount. Of course, if you are juicing for a family simply multiply the recipe accordingly.

You can enhance and vary the flavour of fruit juice by adding fresh ginger, the grated rind of lemons or oranges, freshly chopped herbs (such as mint, sage and thyme) or spices (such as nutmeg, cinnamon and mixed spice). Refer to 'Herbs and Spices for Juicing' on page 168 for useful information and tips.

You will find recipes in this section listed under their dominant ingre-dient (for example, Apple and Orange Juice appears under 'Apple').

Apple

Nutrients per 100 g/3¹/₂ oz

Protein	0.2 g
Fat	0.6 g
Carbohydrate	14.5 g
Calcium	7 mg
Phosphorus	10 mg
Magnesium	8 mg
Iron	0.3 mg
Sodium	1 mg
Potassium	110 mg
Vitamin A	90 mg
Vitamin B1	0.03 IU
Vitamin B2	0.02 mg
Vitamin B3	0.1 mg
Vitamin C	4 mg
kJ	222
Calories	53

Apples have always been highly regarded as a healthy food. That age-old rhyme 'an apple a day keeps the doctor away' could well stem from the fact that the average apple provides nine of the sixteen chemical elements and four of the six most important vitamins required by the human body to function and protect itself against disease.

The health-promoting qualities of apple juice are diverse. It can assist in lowering blood-cholesterol levels, building resistance against infection, changing colonic flora and reducing the colonic bacilli, eliminating body toxins and controlling blood pressure and blood-sugar levels. Because of its high mineral content apple juice is also excellent for producing healthy skin, hair and fingernails. Adding 1 part apple juice to 2 parts milk is believed to reduce the tendency to produce milk-forming mucus in susceptible people.

The fruit acids of the apple stimulate the digestion process and assist in the assimilation of nutrients. The large amount of fruit pectin found in the juice forms a gel in the intestines that absorbs and dissolves toxins and normalises the process of elimination. It is widely recognised that apple juice provides the safest, most immediate and symptomatic relief from diarrhoea and bowel infections; is especially safe for treating infants with these disorders.

Anti-cancer chemicals are found in the skin of apples, so always juice unpeeled fruit. Also, an unpeeled apple yields twice as much vitamin A as a peeled apple.

All apple varieties juice well and make refreshing and delicious drinks. The hard, crisp apple produces the most juice, the flavour of which is sweet and delicate. Over-ripe apples tend to have a stronger taste and the juice breaks up more easily, resulting in a soupy mixture.

Before juicing, wash the apples thoroughly, remove the cores and cut the fruit to fit the juicer. If the apples have been waxed you should peel them before juicing.

Apple Juice

450 g/1 lb apples

- Wash the apples and remove the cores.
- Cut the apples to fit the juicer.
- Push the fruit through the juicer using the safety plunger.

Apple juice can be diluted 1 part apple juice to $1/2$–1 part water.

Apple and Carrot Juice

300 g/10½ oz apples
100 g/3½ oz carrots

- Wash the apples and remove the cores.
- Using a soft brush under a running tap, remove any dirt from the carrots. Don't peel them as most of the vital nutrients are found in and just under the skin.
- Cut the apples and carrots to fit the juicer.
- Push the apple and carrot through the juicer using the safety plunger.

Apple, Carrot and Beetroot Juice

200 g/ 7 oz apples
200 g/ 7 oz carrots
50 g/2 oz beetroot

- Wash the apples and remove the cores.
- Using a soft brush under a running tap, remove any dirt from the carrots and beetroot.
- Cut the apples, carrots and beetroot to fit the juicer.
- Push the apple, carrot and beetroot through the juicer using the safety plunger.

A little fresh parsley or fresh basil pushed through the juicer at the end of juicing creates a special flavour.

Apple and Celery Juice

300 g/10½ oz apples
150 g/5 oz celery

- Wash the apples and remove the cores.
- Wash the celery. Do not remove the leaves.
- Cut the apples to fit the juicer.
- Push the apple and celery through the juicer using the safety plunger.

If you have fennel growing in the garden add just a little at the end of juicing for an interesting aniseed flavour.

Apple, Celery and Ginger Juice

300 g/10½ oz apples
150 g/5 oz celery
2 cm/¾ inch piece
  ginger

- Wash the apples and remove the cores.
- Wash the celery. Do not remove the leaves.
- Peel the ginger.
- Cut the apples to fit the juicer.
- Push the apple, celery and ginger through the juicer using the safety plunger.

Apple and Coconut Juice

225 g/8 oz apples
1 coconut

- Wash the apples and remove the cores.
- Open the coconut and measure out 125 ml/ 4 fl oz/½ cup coconut milk (I use a screw-driver to penetrate the soft eye of the coconut – the coconut milk pours out easily).
- Cut the apples to fit the juicer.
- Push the apple through the juicer using the safety plunger.
- Combine the apple juice with the coconut milk.

A pinch of cinnamon or nutmeg on top of this juice varies the flavour of this refreshing drink.

Apple and Cucumber Juice

200 g/7 oz apples
400 g/14 oz cucumber

- Wash the apples and remove the cores.
- Wash the cucumber. Remove the skin if it has a bitter taste.
- Cut the apples and cucumber to fit the juicer.
- Push the apple and cucumber through the juicer using the safety plunger.

A little finely grated lemon rind gives this juice a pleasant tang.

Apple and Grape Juice

250 g/9 oz apples
200 g/7 oz grapes

- Wash the apples and remove the cores.
- Wash the grapes and remove the fruit from the stems.
- Cut the apples to fit the juicer.
- Push the fruit through the juicer using the safety plunger.

Apple and Grapefruit Juice

200 g/ 7 oz apples
300 g/10½ oz grapefruit

- Wash the apples and remove the cores.
- Peel the grapefruit and remove half the white pith from the flesh.
- Cut the apples and grapefruit to fit the juicer.
- Push the fruit through the juicer using the safety plunger.

This is a bitter juice that can be sweetened with ½ teaspoon of honey.

Apple and Lemon Juice

300 g/10½ oz apples
150 g/5 oz lemons

- Wash the apples and remove the cores.
- Peel the lemons and remove half the white pith.
- Cut the fruit to fit the juicer.
- Push the fruit through the juicer using the safety plunger.

Apple and Orange Juice

300 g/10½ oz apples
200 g/ 7 oz oranges

- Wash the apples and remove the cores.
- Peel the oranges and remove half the white pith.
- Cut the apples and oranges to fit the juicer.
- Push the fruit through the juicer using the safety plunger.

This juice can be topped with a little finely grated orange rind and just a pinch of cinnamon.

Apple and Pear Juice

250 g/ 9 oz apples
250 g/ 9 oz pears

- Wash the apples and pears, remove the cores and cut the fruit to fit the juicer.
- Push the fruit through the juicer using the safety plunger.

Serve this juice over lots of ice and sprinkle it with finely chopped fresh mint and a little finely grated lemon rind.

Apple and Strawberry Juice

200 g/ 7 oz apples
200 g/ 7 oz strawberries

- Wash the apples and remove the cores.
- Wash and hull the strawberries.
- Cut the apples to fit the juicer.
- Push the fruit through the juicer using the safety plunger.

Children love this pale-pink juice. It is sweet and loaded with nutrients. Add some mineral water to make it a fizzy surprise at the next birthday party.

Apricot

Nutrients per 100 g/3½ oz

Protein .... 1 g
Fat .... 0.2 g
Carbohydrate .... 12.8 g
Calcium .... 17 mg
Phosphorus ...... 23 mg
Magnesium ...... 12 mg
Iron .... 0.5 mg
Sodium .... 1 mg
Potassium .... 281 mg
Vitamin A ...... 2700 IU
Vitamin B1 ..... 0.03 mg
Vitamin B2 ..... 0.04 mg
Vitamin B3 .... 0.6 mg
Vitamin C .... 10 mg
kJ 188
Calories 45

Apricots have a rather short season so be ready to try some of these delicious juice ideas when the fruit is at its peak.

Apricot juice is highly alkaline. It is prized for its nutrients and is considered an ideal blood builder and purifier. The people of the Hunza Valley in Kashmir, who are well known for their propensity to live long and healthy lives, eat a lot of apricots.

This delicious thick purée is a meal on its own. It can be thinned down with water or other juices. When apricots are not in season soak sundried apricots in water overnight and purée the mixture to make a delicious sweet drink or add it to other fruit juices, such as apple or pear.

Apricot Juice

400 g/14 oz apricots

- Wash the apricots and remove the stones.
- Push the fruit through the juicer using the safety plunger.

Apricot juice can be diluted 1 part juice to 3 parts water. See colour plate opposite page 74.

Apricot and Apple Juice

200 g/7 oz apricots
250 g/9 oz apples

- Wash the apricots and remove the stones.
- Wash the apples, remove the cores and cut the fruit to fit juicer.
- Push the fruit through the juicer using the safety plunger.

Apricot and Coconut Juice

200 g/7 oz apricots
1 coconut

- Wash the apricots and remove the stones.
- Open the coconut and measure out 125 ml/ 4 fl oz/½ cup coconut milk (I use a screwdriver to penetrate the soft eye of the coconut – the milk pours out easily).
- Push the apricots through the juicer using the safety plunger.
- Add the coconut milk to the juice and stir through.

This juice is delicious served with a pinch of nutmeg.

OPPOSITE: Guava Juice (page 76) and Grape Tropicana (page 71).

Apricot and Grape Juice

200 g/7 oz apricots
200 g/7 oz grapes

- Wash the apricots and remove the stones.
- Wash the grapes and remove the fruit from the stems.
- Push the fruit through the juicer using the safety plunger.

As this juice is very sweet you may want to dilute it 1 part juice to 1 part water or mineral water.

Apricot, Mango and Orange Juice

100 g/3¹/₂ oz apricots
150 g/5 oz mango flesh
200 g/7 oz oranges

- Wash the apricots and remove the stones.
- Cut the mango flesh to fit the juicer.
- Peel the oranges, leaving half the white pith, and cut to fit the juicer.
- Push the fruit through the juicer using the safety plunger.

Apricot and Orange Juice

200 g/7 oz apricots
200 g/7 oz oranges

- Wash the apricots and remove the stones.
- Peel the oranges, leaving half the white pith, and cut to fit the juicer.
- Push the fruit through the juicer using the safety plunger.

OPPOSITE: Berry Bloom (page 63).

Apricot and Pineapple Juice

200 g/ 7 oz apricots
200 g/ 7 oz pineapple
flesh

- Wash the apricots and remove the stones.
- Trim any skin from the pineapple and cut the flesh to fit the juicer.
- Push the fruit through the juicer using the safety plunger.

This juice can be diluted 1 part juice to 1 part water or mineral water.

Apricot Tropical

100 g/3¹/₂ oz apricots
150 g/5 oz mango or
papaw flesh
100 g/3¹/₂ oz pineapple
flesh
150 g/5 oz apples
1–2 passionfruit

- Wash the apricots and remove the stones.
- Remove any remaining skin from the mango and pineapple and cut the fruit to fit the juicer.
- Wash the apples, remove the cores and cut the fruit to fit the juicer.
- Cut the passionfruit in half and scoop out the juice and pulp.
- Push the apricots, mango, pineapple and apple through the juicer using the safety plunger.
- Add the passionfruit juice and pulp to the fruit juice and stir through.

For a special treat, serve this in a pineapple shell decorated lavishly with tropical fruits.

Banana

Nutrients per 100 g/3½ oz

Protein .... 1.1 g
Fat .... 0.2 g
Carbohydrate .... 22.2 g
Calcium .... 8 mg
Phosphorus ...... 26 mg
Magnesium ...... 33 mg
Iron .... 0.7 mg
Sodium .... 1 mg
Potassium .... 370 mg
Vitamin A .... 190 mg
Vitamin B1 ...... 0.05 IU
Vitamin B2 ..... 0.06 mg
Vitamin B3 .... 0.7 mg
Vitamin C .... 10 mg
kJ 364
Calories 87

Bananas, in fact, do not juice well. The best way to 'juice' a banana is to soak it in water overnight before puréeing the mixture or to make a smoothie (see pages 157–162).

Ripe bananas are an alkaline-forming food containing all six of the important vitamins and are especially rich in potassium. The high fruit-sugar level of bananas makes them an ideal energy food.

Banana Juice

1 banana
250 ml/8 fl oz/1 cup
  water
½–1 lemon
cinnamon

- Peel the banana and slice.
- Cover the fruit with water and leave to stand overnight or for at least 6 hours.
- Purée the mixture.
- Add lemon juice and cinnamon to taste.

Blueberry

Nutrients per 100 g/3½ oz

Protein .... 0.7 g
Fat .... 0.5 g
Carbohydrate .... 15.3 g
Calcium .... 15 mg
Phosphorus ...... 13 mg
Magnesium .... 6 mg
Iron .... 1 mg
Sodium .... 1 mg
Potassium .... 81 mg
Vitamin A .... 100 IU
Vitamin B1 ..... 0.03 mg
Vitamin B2 ..... 0.06 mg
Vitamin B3 .... 0.5 mg
Vitamin C .... 14 mg
kJ 240
Calories 58

Though very small, these dark-blue berries have a big taste. They are high in vitamins A and C and contain moderate amounts of iron and fibre. The energy source of blueberries comes from carbohydrate. Blueberries yield a deliciously thick, sweet juice. Always choose just-ripe berries with firm skins for juicing.

Blueberry Juice

400 g/14 oz blueberries
- Wash the blueberries.
- Push the fruit through the juicer using the safety plunger.

Blueberry juice can be diluted 1 part juice to 1–2 parts water.

Blueberry and Apple Juice

200 g/ 7 oz blueberries
200 g/ 7 oz apples

- Wash the blueberries.
- Wash the apples, remove the cores and cut the fruit to fit the juicer.
- Push the fruit through the juicer using the safety plunger.

Blueberry, Nectarine and Apple Juice

100 g/3¹/₂ oz blueberries
200 g/ 7 oz nectarines
200 g/ 7 oz apples

- Wash the blueberries.
- Wash the nectarines, remove the stones and cut the fruit to fit the juicer.
- Wash the apples, remove the cores and cut the fruit to fit the juicer.
- Push the fruit through the juicer using the safety plunger.

Blueberry, Pear and Lemon Juice

200 g/ 7 oz blueberries
250 g/ 9 oz pears
1–2 tablespoons lemon
juice

- Wash the blueberries.
- Wash the pears, remove the cores and cut the fruit to fit the juicer.
- Push the fruit through the juicer using the safety plunger.
- Add the lemon juice to the fruit juice and stir through.

Berry Bloom

200 g/ 7 oz blueberries
100 g/3¹/₂ oz raspberries
125 g/4¹/₂ oz strawberries

- Wash the blueberries and raspberries.
- Wash and hull the strawberries.
- Push all the berries through the juicer using the safety plunger.

See colour plate opposite page 59.

Blueberry Tutti Fruiti

100 g/3¹/₂ oz blueberries
180 g/6 oz kiwifruit
100 g/3¹/₂ oz apple
125 g/4¹/₂ oz pear

- Wash the blueberries.
- Peel the furry skin from the kiwifruit and cut the fruit to fit the juicer.
- Wash the apple, remove the core and cut the fruit to fit the juicer.
- Wash the pear, remove the core and cut the fruit to fit the juicer.
- Push the fruit through the juicer using the safety plunger.

Cantaloup

Nutrients per 100 g/3½ oz

Protein .... 0.7 g
Fat .... 0.1 g
Carbohydrate ...... 7.5 g
Calcium .... 14 mg
Phosphorus ...... 16 mg
Magnesium ...... 16 mg
Iron .... 0.4 mg
Sodium .... 12 mg
Potassium .... 251 mg
Vitamin A ...... 3400 IU
Vitamin B1 ..... 0.04 mg
Vitamin B2 ..... 0.03 mg
Vitamin B3 .... 0.6 mg
Vitamin C .... 33 mg
kJ 142
Calories 34

Cantaloup (also called rockmelons) make delicious, thirst-quenching and high-energy juice, as do honeydew melons and watermelons. However, it has often been said that melons should be eaten alone or left alone: melons combine well with other melons but can cause indigestion when mixed with other foods.

Cantaloup are especially rich in vitamins A, B complex and C, as are honeydew melons. Cantaloup tend to create a diuretic effect (they eliminate excess fluids from the body) and act as a natural laxative. Because of this 'flushing' nature melons help move wastes away from the skin and nourish it with their rich nutrients.

Cantaloup Juice

350 g/12 oz cantaloup

- Peel the cantaloup and remove the seeds. Cut the melon to fit the juicer.
- Push the melon through the juicer using the safety plunger.

Melon juice can be diluted 1 part juice to 1 part water.

Cantaloup and Ginger Tonic

350 g/12 oz cantaloup
4 cm/1½ inch piece
  ginger

- Peel the cantaloup and remove the seeds.
- Cut the melon to fit the juicer.
- Peel the ginger.
- Push the melon and ginger through the juicer using the safety plunger.

For a different taste sensation, try using honeydew melon or watermelon instead of cantaloup.

Three Melon Cocktail

150 g/5 oz cantaloup
150 g/5 oz honeydew
  melon
150 g/5 oz watermelon

- Peel the melons and remove the seeds (watermelon skin, which is high in chlorophyll, can be juiced if desired).
- Cut the melons to fit the juicer.
- Push the melon through the juicer using the safety plunger.

Fig

Nutrients per 100 g/3½ oz	
Protein	1.2 g
Fat	0.3 g
Carbohydrate	20.3 g
Calcium	35 mg
Phosphorus	22 mg
Magnesium	20 mg
Iron	0.6 mg
Sodium	2 mg
Potassium	194 mg
Vitamin A	80 IU
Vitamin B1	0.06 mg
Vitamin B2	0.05 mg
Vitamin B3	0.4 mg
Vitamin C	2 mg
kJ	318
Calories	76

The pulpy sweet flesh of this deep-purple fruit yields an unusual, thick and somewhat fragrant juice. It is nectar-like and almost too thick to drink on its own; try mixing it with a variety of other juices to create wonderful fruit cocktails.

Fig juice is good energy food and it contains moderate amounts of most nutrients. Select soft, plump and brightly coloured fruit with undamaged skins. They should smell sweet and fragrant. If a fig has a sour smell it is over-ripe and not suitable for juicing.

Fig Juice

400 g/14 oz figs

- Wash the figs and remove the stems.
- Push the fruit through the juicer using the safety plunger.

Fig juice can be diluted 1 part juice to 3 parts water.

Fig and Apple Juice

200 g/7 oz figs
200 g/7 oz apples

- Wash the figs and remove the stems.
- Wash the apples, remove the cores and cut the fruit to fit the juicer.
- Push the fruit through the juicer using the safety plunger.

Fig and Grape Juice

200 g/7 oz figs
200 g/7 oz grapes

- Wash the figs and remove the stems.
- Wash the grapes and remove the fruit from the stems.
- Push the fruit through the juicer using the safety plunger.

Grape

Nutrients per 100 g/3½ oz

Protein	1.3 g
Fat	0.1 g
Carbohydrate	15.7 g
Calcium	16 mg
Phosphorus	12 mg
Magnesium	13 mg
Iron	0.4 mg
Sodium	3 mg
Potassium	158 mg
Vitamin A	100 mg
Vitamin B1	0.05 IU
Viamin B2	0.03 mg
Vitamin B3	0.3 mg
Vitamin C	4 mg
kJ	276
Calories	66

For centuries grape-juice diets have been used to treat cancer and many other chronic illnesses in an attempt to bring about healing and wellbeing. As part of a cleansing and revitalising therapy grape juice is taken for several days or even weeks.

Grape juice is rich in nutrients and high in energy. The minerals found in grapes help to cleanse and build the blood while stimulating the liver to increase its cleansing activity. Grape juice also lowers the blood-acidity level. Other health benefits associated with grape juice include improved blood circulation, lowered blood pressure, skin cleansing and nourishing, liver revitalisation, improved rheumatism and arthritis, and increased energy levels and weight loss. Taken last thing at night, grape juice has also been credited with promoting good sleep.

The seedless varieties of grapes are best used for juicing. The berries should be fresh, firm and plump.

Grape Juice

350–400 g/12–14 oz grapes

- Wash the grapes and remove the fruit from the stems.
- Push the grapes through the juicer using the safety plunger.

Grape juice can be diluted 1 part grape juice to ½–1 part water.

Grape, Apple and Lemon Juice

200 g/7 oz grapes
150 g/5 oz apples
2 tablespoons lemon juice

- Wash the grapes and remove the fruit from the stems.
- Wash the apples, remove the cores and cut the fruit to fit the juicer.
- Push the fruit through the juicer using the safety plunger.
- Add the lemon juice to the fruit juice and stir through.

For a flavour variation, try adding a small piece of fresh peeled ginger to the juicer.

Grape and Kiwifruit Juice

200 g/7 oz purple grapes
250 g/9 oz kiwifruit

- Wash the grapes and remove the fruit from the stems.
- Peel the furry skin from the kiwifruit and cut the fruit to fit the juicer.
- Push the fruit through the juicer using the safety plunger.

To give this juice a rather special taste add just a little finely grated lemon rind and some very finely chopped fresh mint. The juice can be served over lots of ice.

Grape and Pear Juice

200 g/ 7 oz grapes
250 g/ 9 oz pears

- Wash the grapes and remove the fruit from the stems.
- Wash the pears, remove the cores and cut the fruit to fit the juicer.
- Push the fruit through the juicer using the safety plunger.

Grape Tropicana

100 g/3¹/₂ oz grapes
100 g/3¹/₂ oz orange
100 g/3¹/₂ oz pineapple
  flesh
90 g/3 oz kiwifruit
1 passionfruit

- Wash the grapes and remove the fruit from the stems.
- Peel the orange, leaving about half the white pith, and cut to fit the juicer.
- Cut the pineapple flesh to fit the juicer.
- Peel the furry skin from the kiwifruit and cut the fruit to fit the juicer.
- Cut the passionfruit in half and scoop out the juice and pulp.
- Push the grapes, orange, pineapple flesh and kiwifruit through the juicer using the safety plunger.
- Add the passionfruit juice and pulp to the fruit juice and stir through.

This juice is delicious and refreshing served over lots of crushed ice. It can also become a party punch by adding 1 part mineral water to 1 part juice. See colour plate opposite page 58.

Grapefruit

Nutrients per 100 g/3½ oz

Protein .... 0.5 g
Fat .... 0.1 g
Carbohydrate .... 10.6 g
Calcium .... 16 mg
Phosphorus ...... 16 mg
Magnesium ...... 12 mg
Iron .... 0.4 mg
Sodium .... 1 mg
Potassium .... 135 mg
Vitamin A .... 80 mg
Vitamin B1 ...... 0.04 IU
Vitamin B2 ..... 0.02 mg
Vitamin B3 .... 0.2 mg
Vitamin C .... 38 mg
kJ 155
Calories 37

It is thought that grapefruit contain an enzyme that stimulates the body's metabolism – hence its popularity on most weight-loss programmes.

There are different varieties of grapefruit and some are sweeter than others. Their commercial origins began in Florida from where we get the popular Florida Duncan, a variety that is particularly good for juicing. The Texan Pink, from the plantations of Texas, is one of the sweeter fruits. The pink and red-fleshed varieties are not only sweeter but are also less acidic than those with white flesh. Other common varieties include the Marsh, the Thompson and the Wheeney.

Firm, bright-yellow fruit that feel heavy will yield the highest quantity of juice. Simply remove the peel, quarter the grapefruit, leaving some of the white pith, and push the fruit through the juicer. Juice made in this way is creamy in texture and full of vital nutrients.

Bioflavonoids, which help the body to retain and use vitamin C, are concentrated in the white pith that surrounds the flesh. These nutrients improve the permeability and strength of the capillary walls, which is particularly important in the latter stages of pregnancy as the capillary walls are commonly stressed by fluid retention and swelling.

Although very nutritious and high in vitamin C, grapefruit juice is high in acid. It is best to drink small amounts or to dilute grapefruit juice with water or other juices. The younger and the more active you are the higher your metabolism and your body's ability to break down acid. For older, less active people grapefruit juice should be drunk in moderation.

The grapefruit and its juice can aid in weight reduction, the lowering of blood pressure, improving a sluggish liver, rapid healing of bruises, skin cleansing and the easing of arthritis. It can also help battle coughs, break up mucus and eliminate catarrh, and fight colds, fevers and sore throats. Taken first thing in the morning grapefruit juice helps to promote easy bowel movement and prevents constipation. Taken last thing at night it helps to induce sleep.

Grapefruit Juice

600 g/1 lb 5 oz grapefruit

- Peel the grapefruit, leaving about half the white pith, and cut the fruit to fit the juicer.
- Push the grapefruit through the juicer.

Grapefruit juice can be diluted 1 part juice to 1–2 parts water.

Grapefruit and Apple Juice

150 g/5 oz grapefruit
300 g/10½ oz apples

- Peel the grapefruit, leaving about half the white pith, and cut the fruit to fit the juicer.
- Wash the apples, remove the cores and cut the fruit to fit the juicer.
- Push the fruit through the juicer using the safety plunger.

As this juice has a fairly bitter taste, try adding ½ teaspoon honey to sweeten it.

Grapefruit and Kiwifruit Juice

150 g/5 oz grapefruit
500 g/1 lb 2 oz kiwifruit

- Peel the grapefruit, leaving about half the white pith, and cut the fruit to fit the juicer.
- Peel the furry skin from the kiwifruit and cut the fruit to fit the juicer.
- Push the fruit through the juicer using the safety plunger.

You might like to add a small piece of peeled fresh ginger to the juicer to give this juice a touch of spice.

Grapefruit and Orange Juice

150 g/5 oz grapefruit
300 g/10½ oz oranges

- Peel the grapefruit and oranges, leaving about half the white pith, and cut the fruit to fit the juicer.
- Push the fruit through the juicer using the safety plunger.

This is a delicious breakfast juice. Served over ice it can be drunk any time you feel like a freshing tonic.

Grapefruit and Pineapple Juice

150 g/5 oz grapefruit
300 g/10½ oz pineapple
flesh

- Peel the grapefruit, leaving about half the white pith, and cut the fruit to fit the juicer.
- Cut the pineapple flesh to fit the juicer.
- Push the fruit through the juicer using the safety plunger.

This is a refreshing juice that can be served over ice with a little finely chopped pineapple sage or mint as a garnish.

OPPOSITE: Pear, Apple and Ginger Juice (page 94) and Apricot Juice (page 58).

Guava

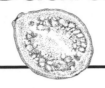

Nutrients per 100 g/3½ oz

Protein	0.8 g
Fat	0.6 g
Carbohydrate	15 g
Calcium	23 mg
Phosphorus	42 mg
Magnesium	13 mg
Iron	0.9 mg
Sodium	4 mg
Potassium	289 mg
Vitamin A	280 IU
Vitamin B1	0.05 mg
Viamin B2	0.05 mg
Vitamin B3	1.2 mg
Vitamin C	242 mg
kJ	264
Calories	63

The guava produces a white to salmon-pink juice that is fruit-salad-like in flavour. It is high in potassium and vitamins A and C. Guava juice is delicious to drink on its own and it also combines well with many other fruits to make wonderful tropical-tasting juices.

The best guava to juice will have a greenish yellow skin and be firm to the touch without soft spots or blemishes.

OPPOSITE: Carrot, Cucumber and Ginger Juice (page 126) and Beetroot, Pineapple and Cucumber Juice (page 114).

Guava Juice

700 g/1 lb 9 oz guava

- Peel the guava and cut the fruit to fit the juicer.
- Push the guava through the juicer using the safety plunger.

Guava juice can be diluted 1 part juice to ½–1 part water. See colour plate opposite page 58.

Guava and Apple Juice

350 g/12 oz guava
200 g/7 oz apples

- Peel the guava and cut the fruit to fit the juicer.
- Wash the apples, remove the cores and cut the fruit to fit the juicer.
- Push the fruit through the juicer using the safety plunger.

Guava Heaven

175 g/6 oz guava
100 g/3½ oz grapes
100 g/3½ oz apple
100 g/3½ oz orange

- Peel the guava and cut to fit the juicer.
- Wash the grapes and remove the fruit from the stems.
- Wash the apple, remove the core and cut the fruit to fit the juicer.
- Peel the orange, leaving about half the white pith, and cut to fit the juicer.
- Push the fruit through the juicer using the safety plunger.

Guava and Pear Juice

350 g/12 oz guava
250 g/9 oz pears

- Peel the guava and cut to fit the juicer.
- Wash the pears, remove the cores and cut the fruit to fit the juicer.
- Push the fruit through the juicer using the safety plunger.

Kiwifruit

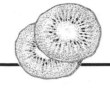

Nutrients per 100 g/3½ oz

Protein .... 0.8 g
Fat .... 0.2 g
Carbohydrate ...... 9.7 g
Calcium .... 18 mg
Phosphorus ...... 15 mg
Magnesium .... 9 mg
Iron .... 0.5 mg
Sodium .... 1 mg
Potassium .... 155 mg
Vitamin A .... 290 mg
Vitamin B1 .... –
Viamin B2 .... –
Vitamin B3 .... –
Vitamin C .... 33 mg
kJ 180
Calories 43

Just one kiwifruit contains enough vitamin C for the recommended daily intake and a moderate amount of iron. Kiwifruit are very low in kilijoules and the delicate juice is sweet.

Kiwifruit Juice

700 g/1 lb 9 oz kiwifruit

- Peel the furry skin from the kiwifruit and cut the fruit to fit the juicer.
- Push the fruit through the juicer using the safety plunger.

Kiwifruit juice can be diluted 1 part juice to ½–1 part water.

Kiwifruit and Apple Juice

350 g/12 oz kiwifruit
200 g/7 oz apples

- Peel the furry skin from the kiwifruit and cut the fruit to fit the juicer.
- Wash the apples, remove the cores and cut the fruit to fit the juicer.
- Push the fruit through the juicer using the safety plunger.

Kiwifruit and Passionfruit Juice

700 g/1 lb 9 oz kiwifruit
2–3 passionfruit

- Peel the furry skin from the kiwifruit and cut the fruit to fit the juicer.
- Cut the passionfruit in halves and scoop out the juice and pulp.
- Push the kiwifruit through the juicer using the safety plunger.
- Add the passionfruit juice and pulp to the kiwifruit juice and stir through.

Kiwifruit and Peach Juice

600 g/1 lb 5 oz kiwifruit
150 g/5 oz peach

- Peel the furry skin from the kiwifruit and cut the fruit to fit the juicer.
- Wash the peach, remove the stone and cut the fruit to fit the juicer.
- Push the fruit through the juicer using the safety plunger.

Kiwifruit and Pear Juice

350 g/12 oz kiwifruit
250 g/9 oz pears

- Peel the furry skin from the kiwifruit and cut the fruit to fit the juicer.
- Wash the pears, remove the cores and cut the fruit to fit the juicer.
- Push the fruit through the juicer using the safety plunger.

Lemon

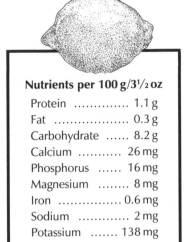

Nutrients per 100 g/3½ oz	
Protein	1.1 g
Fat	0.3 g
Carbohydrate	8.2 g
Calcium	26 mg
Phosphorus	16 mg
Magnesium	8 mg
Iron	0.6 mg
Sodium	2 mg
Potassium	138 mg
Vitamin A	20 mg
Vitamin B1	0.04 IU
Viamin B2	0.02 mg
Vitamin B3	0.1 mg
Vitamin C	53 mg
kJ	134
Calories	32

The lemon contains the highest amount of vitamin C of all the fruit in the citrus family and is highly regarded for its medicinal values. Like the grapefruit it is high in acid so should be taken in moderation or diluted with water. One part lemon juice to 2 or 3 parts water is a good mix. If you find the juice too bitter add a little honey.

Lemon juice is effective as a mild laxative and blood purifier. It promotes the secretion of bile and is believed to prevent the formation of acid deposits and gallstones. Diluted with water and sipped slowly, it may be beneficial in overcoming nausea. Sipped straight, it relieves sore throats, coughs, colds, catarrh, bronchitis, asthma and the flu. Its anti-bacterial action not only soothes but also helps fight the infection related to these illnesses. However, lemon juice should *not* be used when the digestive or intestinal tract is inflamed.

Lemon juice is also a very effective anti-oxidant. A diet rich in anti-oxidants is the best way to protect ourselves against heart disease, cancer and other such illnesses. Anti-oxidants appear to be the main destroyers of the free radicals that occur naturally in our body and that are the residue of pollution, cigarettes and the sun's radiation. These free radicals create changes at a cellular level that hasten ageing and promote an environment ripe for the development of disease, senility and eye cataracts.

Choose lemons that are bright-yellow, heavy and that have a firm, textured skin. These will yield the most juice. If lemons have thin skins it is not necessary to peel them. Limes can be substituted when lemons are not available.

Lemon Juice

450 g/1 lb lemons

- Wash the lemons and peel them, leaving half the white pith, if the skins are thick or have been waxed.
- Cut the lemons to fit the juicer.
- Push the fruit through the juicer using the safety plunger.

Lemon juice can be diluted 1 part juice to 2–3 parts water.

Lemon, Apple and Mint Juice

150 g/5 oz lemons
300 g/10¹/₂ oz apples
few sprigs of mint

- Wash the lemons and peel them, leaving half the white pith, if the skins are thick or have been waxed.
- Cut the lemons to fit the juicer.
- Wash the apples, remove the cores and cut the fruit to fit the juicer.
- Push the fruit and mint through the juicer using the safety plunger.

Lemon, Blueberry and Pear Juice

100 g/3¹/₂ oz lemons
200 g/7 oz blueberries
250 g/9 oz pears

- Wash the lemons and peel them, leaving half the white pith, if the skins are thick or have been waxed.
- Cut the lemons to fit the juicer.
- Wash the blueberries.
- Wash the pears and remove the cores.
- Cut the pears to fit the juicer.
- Push the fruit through the juicer using the safety plunger.

Lemon, Celery and Ginger Juice

150 g/5 oz lemons
300 g/10¹/₂ oz celery
2.5 cm/1 inch piece ginger

- Wash the lemons and peel them, leaving half the white pith, if the skins are thick or have been waxed.
- Cut the lemons to fit the juicer.
- Wash the celery. Do not remove the foliage.
- Peel the ginger.
- Push the lemon, celery and ginger through the juicer using the safety plunger.

Lemon and Grape Juice

150 g/5 oz lemons
200 g/7 oz grapes

- Wash the lemons and peel them, leaving half the white pith, if the skins are thick or have been waxed.
- Cut the lemons to fit the juicer.
- Wash the grapes and remove the fruit from the stems.
- Push the fruit through the juicer using the safety plunger.

Try adding a little grated fresh nutmeg to this juice for a hint of spice.

Lemon, Mandarin and Pineapple Juice

150 g/5 oz lemons
200 g/7 oz mandarins
100 g/3½ oz pineapple flesh

- Wash the lemons and peel them, leaving half the white pith, if the skins are thick or have been waxed.
- Cut the lemons to fit the juicer.
- Peel the mandarins and segment the fruit to fit the juicer.
- Cut the pineapple to fit the juicer.
- Push the fruit through the juicer using the safety plunger.

Lemon and Orange Juice

150 g/5 oz lemons
300 g/10½ oz oranges

- Wash the lemons and peel them, leaving half the white pith, if the skins are thick or have been waxed.
- Cut the lemons to fit the juicer.
- Peel the oranges, leaving half the white pith, and cut to fit the juicer.
- Push the fruit through the juicer using the safety plunger.

Lemon, Strawberry and Apple Juice

100 g/3½ oz lemons
250 g/9 oz strawberries
200 g/7 oz apples

- Wash the lemons and peel them, leaving half the white pith, if the skins are thick or have been waxed.
- Cut the lemons to fit the juicer.
- Wash and hull the strawberries.
- Wash the apples, remove the cores and cut the fruit to fit the juicer.
- Push the fruit through the juicer using the safety plunger.

Mango

Nutrients per 100 g/3½ oz

Protein	0.7 g
Fat	0.4 g
Carbohydrate	16.8 g
Calcium	10 mg
Phosphorus	13 mg
Magnesium	18 mg
Iron	0.4 mg
Sodium	7 mg
Potassium	189 mg
Vitamin A	4800 IU
Vitamin B1	0.05 mg
Viamin B2	0.05 mg
Vitamin B3	1.1 mg
Vitamin C	35 mg
kJ	276
Calories	66

Mangoes have been referred to as 'the fruit of the gods' and their juice as 'God's nectar'. Mango juice is bright orange, slightly aromatic and spicy and even a little peachy in flavour. It is almost too thick to drink on its own but it combines well with many other fruit juices.

Like the kiwifruit, one mango provides the daily recommended intake of vitamin C. It is also rich in beta-carotene, the plant form of vitamin A.

Choose mangoes that have smooth and firm but soft skins. If ripe, a mango will have a fragrant aroma and will yield if pressed gently. To ripen the fruit store it at room temperature. To juice, simply peel away the skin and cut the flesh away from the stone.

Mango Juice

600 g / 1 lb 5 oz mango
flesh

- Cut the mango to fit the juicer.
- Push the fruit through the juicer using the safety plunger.

Mango juice can be diluted 1 part juice to 3 parts water. You will need 2 mangoes to obtain 600 g/1 lb 5 oz flesh.

Mango and Coconut Juice

300 g / 10½ oz mango
flesh
1 coconut

- Cut the mango to fit the juicer.
- Push the mango through the juicer using the safety plunger.
- Open the coconut and measure out 125 ml/ 4 fl oz / ½ cup coconut milk (I use a screwdriver to penetrate the soft eye of the coconut – the milk pours out easily).
- Add the coconut milk to the mango juice and stir through.

For an extra scrumptious juice add some grated fresh coconut to the glass.

Mango and Kiwifruit Juice

300 g / 10½ oz mango
flesh
350 g / 12 oz kiwifruit

- Cut the mango to fit the juicer.
- Peel the furry skin from the kiwifruit and cut the fruit to fit the juicer.
- Push the fruit through the juicer using the safety plunger.

Mango and Orange Juice

300 g / 10½ oz mango
flesh
200 g / 7 oz oranges

- Cut the mango to fit the juicer.
- Peel the oranges, leaving half the white pith, and cut to fit the juicer.
- Push the fruit through the juicer using the safety plunger.

Mango Tease

300 g/10¹/₂ oz mango flesh
200 g/7 oz oranges
1–2 tablespoons lemon juice

- Cut the mango to fit the juicer.
- Peel the oranges, leaving half the white pith, and cut to fit the juicer.
- Push the fruit through the juicer using the safety plunger.
- Add the lemon juice to the fruit juice to taste and stir through.

Mango Tropicana

150 g/5 oz mango flesh
100 g/3¹/₂ oz orange
200 g/7 oz pineapple flesh
1–2 passionfruit

- Cut the mango to fit the juicer.
- Peel the orange, leaving half the white pith, and cut to fit the juicer.
- Cut the pineapple to fit the juicer.
- Cut the passionfruit in halves and scoop out the juice and the pulp.
- Push the mango, orange and pineapple through the juicer using the safety plunger.
- Add the passionfruit juice and pulp to the fruit juice and stir through.

This juice can easily be made into a punch by adding 1 part juice to 1–2 parts mineral water.

Orange

Nutrients per 100 g/3½ oz

Protein	1 g
Fat	0.2 g
Carbohydrate	12.2 g
Calcium	41 mg
Phosphorus	20 mg
Magnesium	11 mg
Iron	0.4 mg
Sodium	1 mg
Potassium	200 mg
Vitamin A	200 IU
Vitamin B1	0.1 mg
Viamin B2	0.04 mg
Vitamin B3	0.4 mg
Vitamin C	50 mg
kJ	188
Calories	45

It may seem easier to buy orange juice at the supermarket, however most commercial juices are made from concentrates that have been pasteurised. This process not only destroys a lot of the vitamin C but it also kills the enzymes. Many commercial juices also contain added sugar and even colour enhancers.

An average-sized orange supplies as much as twice the daily recommended amount of vitamin C and is rich in a wide variety of nutrients. Its health benefits are similar to the lemon and grapefruit. It cleanses and tones the gastro-intestinal tract and improves the permeability and strength of the capillary walls. It fights colds, fever and influenza and is helpful in treating asthma, bronchitis, catarrh, blood disorders, anaemia, scurvy, heart disease, high blood pressure, indigestion, liver disorders, lung disorders, pneumonia and skin disorders and can aid weight loss.

Orange juice is also an excellent source of calcium and phosphorus. It assists in the formation of bones and teeth and prevents rickets.

Orange juice can be given to infants from 3 weeks. Juicing oranges in a juice machine is ideal for infants because it removes the fibre, which is too aggressive on their small bowels. Fibre-free juice is also richer in nutrients than juice from a squeezed orange because the pith, which contains cancer-preventing bioflavonoids (see pages 9 and 39), is juiced as well. It is best to introduce infants to diluted orange juice first – 1 part juice to 1 part water is a suitable ratio. Start with 2 or 3 teaspoonfuls each day, slowly increasing the amount. From the age of 4–6 months infants should be taking at least 2 tablespoons twice or three times daily.

Orange Juice

400 g/14 oz oranges

- Peel the oranges, leaving half the white pith, and cut to fit the juicer.
- Push the fruit through the juicer using the safety plunger.

Orange juice can be diluted 1 part juice to 1 part water.

Orange, Apple and Mango Juice

200 g/7 oz oranges
150 g/5 oz apples
150 g/5 oz mango flesh

- Peel the oranges, leaving half the white pith, and cut to fit the juicer.
- Wash the apples, remove the cores and cut the fruit to fit the juicer.
- Cut the mango flesh to fit the juicer.
- Push the fruit through the juicer using the safety plunger.

Orange and Guava Juice

200 g/7 oz oranges
350 g/12 oz guava

- Peel the oranges, leaving about half the white pith, and cut to fit the juicer.
- Peel the guava and cut to fit the juicer.
- Push the fruit through the juicer using the safety plunger.

Orange and Lemon Juice

300 g/10¹/₂ oz oranges
150 g/5 oz lemons

- Peel the oranges, leaving half the white pith, and cut to fit the juicer.
- Wash the lemons and peel them, leaving half the white pith, if the skins are thick or have been waxed. Cut the lemons to fit the juicer.
- Push the fruit through the juicer using the safety plunger.

Orange Passion Juice

400 g/14 oz oranges
2–3 passionfruit

- Peel the oranges, leaving half the white pith, and cut to fit the juicer.
- Cut the passionfruit in halves and scoop out the juice and pulp.
- Push the orange through the juicer using the safety plunger.
- Add the passionfruit to the orange juice and stir through.

Orange and Pineapple Juice

300 g/10¹/₂ oz oranges
200 g/7 oz pineapple
  flesh

- Peel the oranges, leaving half the white pith, and cut to fit the juicer.
- Cut the pineapple to fit the juicer.
- Push the fruit through the juicer using the safety plunger.

Orange Berry Tango

200 g/ 7 oz oranges
250 g/ 9 oz strawberries
1–2 tablespoons lemon
juice

- Peel the oranges, leaving half the white pith, and cut to fit the juicer.
- Wash and hull the strawberries.
- Push the orange and strawberries through the juicer using a safety plunger.
- Add the lemon juice to the fruit juice to taste and stir through.

Orange Island Cooler

100 g/3¹/₂ oz orange
100 g/3¹/₂ oz pineapple
flesh
100 g/3¹/₂ oz mandarin
150 g/5 oz apples
1–2 passionfruit

- Peel the orange, leaving half the white pith, and cut to fit the juicer.
- Cut the pineapple to fit the juicer.
- Peel the mandarin and segment the fruit to fit the juicer.
- Wash the apples, remove the cores and cut the fruit to fit the juicer.
- Cut the passionfruit in halves and scoop out the juice and pulp.
- Push the orange, pineapple, mandarin and apple through the juicer using the safety plunger.
- Add the passionfruit juice and pulp to the fruit juice and stir through.

This juice can be easily made into a refreshing punch by adding 1 part juice to 1 part mineral water.

Peach

Nutrients per 100 g/3½ oz

Protein .... 0.6 g
Fat .... 0.1 g
Carbohydrate ...... 9.7 g
Calcium .... 9 mg
Phosphorus ...... 19 mg
Magnesium ...... 10 mg
Iron .... 0.5 mg
Sodium .... 1 mg
Potassium .... 202 mg
Vitamin A ...... 1330 IU
Vitamin B1 ..... 0.02 mg
Viamin B2 ...... 0.05 mg
Vitamin B3 .... 1 mg
Vitamin C .... 7 mg
kJ 172
Calories 41

The heavenly flavour of the peach makes it an ideal fruit to juice. The thick and luscious juice can be diluted with water or any number of other juices.

Peaches are rich in vitamin A. Peach juice is useful in the treatment of anaemia, high blood pressure, gastritis, acidosis, bronchitis, asthma, poor digestion and morning sickness in pregnant women. Peach juice also cleanses the bowel and stimulates peristalsis – the wavelike contractions that bring about easy elimination.

Choose peaches that are fresh and without bruises and ripe enough that they yield when gently touched. The riper the peach, the more nutritious and the sweeter the juice. To prepare peaches for juicing, peel the furry skin (or scrub the skin clean) and cut the flesh away from the stone.

Peach Juice

600/1 lb 5 oz peaches

- Peel the peaches, remove the stones and cut the fruit to fit the juicer.
- Push the fruit through the juicer using the safety plunger.

Peach juice can be diluted 1 part juice to 3 parts water. For a delicious sparkling drink combine 1 part juice and 1 part mineral water and serve over lots of ice.

Peach and Apple Juice

300 g/10¹/₂ oz peaches
200 g/5 oz apples

- Peel the peaches, remove the stones and cut the fruit to fit the juicer.
- Wash the apples, remove the cores and cut the fruit to fit the juicer.
- Push the fruit through the juicer using the safety plunger.

For a variation in flavour try adding a dash of cinnamon to this sweet juice.

Peach, Apple and Cherry Surprise

250 g/9 oz peaches
150 g/5 oz apples
150 g/5 oz cherries

- Peel the peaches, remove the stones and cut the fruit to fit the juicer.
- Wash the apples, remove the cores and cut the fruit to fit the juicer.
- Wash the cherries and remove the stems and pips (a cherry pipper makes this task easier).
- Push the fruit through the juicer using the safety plunger.

Peach, Apricot and Nectarine Juice

300 g/10¹/₂ oz peaches
100 g/3¹/₂ oz apricots
250 g/9 oz nectarines

- Peel the peaches, remove the stones and cut the fruit to fit the juicer.
- Wash the apricots, remove the stones and cut the fruit to fit the juicer.
- Wash the nectarines, remove the stones and cut the fruit to fit the juicer.
- Push the fruit through the juicer using the safety plunger.

This is a particularly fragrant juice that can be sharpened by adding a squeeze of lemon juice or spiced up by mixing through a pinch of cinnamon.

Peach and Guava Juice

300 g/10¹/₂ oz peaches
350 g/12 oz guava

- Peel the peaches, remove the stones and cut the fruit to fit the juicer.
- Peel the guava and cut the fruit to fit the juicer.
- Push the fruit through the juicer using the safety plunger.

Peach and Orange Juice

300 g/10¹/₂ oz peaches
200 g/7 oz oranges

- Peel the peaches, remove the stones and cut the fruit to fit the juicer.
- Peel the oranges, leaving half the white pith, and cut to fit the juicer.
- Push the fruit through the juicer using the safety plunger.

Surprisingly, this juice can be thinned with cucumber juice to make a cool and refreshing summer drink. Dilute the juice 1 part peach and orange juice to 1 part cucumber juice. For a different taste sensation, substitute pineapple for the oranges.

Pear

Nutrients per 100 g/3½ oz

Protein .... 0.7 g
Fat .... 0.4 g
Carbohydrate .... 15.3 g
Calcium .... 8 mg
Phosphorus ...... 11 mg
Magnesium .... 7 mg
Iron .... 0.3 mg
Sodium .... 2 mg
Potassium .... 130 mg
Vitamin A .... 20 mg
Vitamin B1 ..... 0.02 mg
Viamin B2 ...... 0.04 mg
Vitamin B3 .... 0.1 mg
Vitamin C .... 4 mg
kJ 234
Calories 56

There are several varieties of pears and all are excellent to juice as long as they are ripe. The juice is quite thick and can be diluted with water or other juices, such as lemon, apple or guava.

Pear juice is said to be an excellent morning tonic. Its rich supply of easily digested natural sugar converts to energy. Pear juice has a mild diuretic and laxative effect and is helpful in conditions of constipation, bladder problems, poor digestion, high blood pressure, obesity, acidosis, skin disorders, colitis and catarrh.

Choose firm but ripe pears for juicing. It is a good idea to let them sit at room temperature for a day or so to fully ripen. However, overly soft pears do not produce a lot of juice.

Pear Juice

600 g/1 lb 5 oz pears

- Wash the pears, remove the cores and cut the fruit to fit the juicer.
- Push the fruit through the juicer using the safety plunger.

Pear juice can be diluted ½ part juice to 1 part water.

Pear, Apple and Ginger Juice

300 g/10½ oz pears
200/7 oz apples
2.5 cm/1 inch piece
* ginger*

- Wash the pears and apples, remove the cores and cut the fruit to fit the juicer.
- Peel the ginger.
- Push the pear, apple and ginger through the juicer using the safety plunger.

This juice is delicious served over lots of ice on a hot summer's day. See colour plate opposite page 74.

Pear, Apple and Lemon Juice

300 g/10½ oz pears
200 g/7 oz apples
1–2 tablespoons lemon
* juice*

- Wash the pears and apples, remove the cores and cut the fruit to fit the juicer.
- Push the pear and apple through the juicer using the safety plunger.
- Add the lemon juice to the fruit juice to taste and stir through.

Pear, Apple and Pineapple Juice

150 g/5 oz pears
150 g/5 oz apples
200 g/7 oz pineapple
  flesh

- Wash the pears and apples and remove the cores.
- Cut the pears and apples to fit the juicer.
- Cut the pineapple to fit the juicer.
- Push the fruit through the juicer using the safety plunger.

Pear and Apricot Juice

250 g/9 oz pears
200 /7 oz apricots

- Wash the pears, remove the cores and cut the fruit to fit the juicer.
- Wash the apricots and remove the stones.
- Push the fruit through the juicer using the safety plunger.

This is a wonderfully delicious thick juice. For a thinner juice, try diluting it with water, apple or cucumber juice.

Pear and Grapefruit Juice

400 g/14 oz pears
150 g/5 oz grapefruit

- Wash the pears, remove the cores and cut the fruit to fit the juicer.
- Peel the grapefruit, leaving half the white pith, and cut to fit the juicer.
- Push the fruit through the juicer using the safety plunger.

Pear, Grapefruit and Pineapple Juice

250 g/ 9 oz pears
150 g/5 oz grapefruit
100 g/3¹/₂ oz pineapple
  flesh

- Wash the pears, remove the cores and cut the fruit to fit the juicer.
- Peel the grapefruit, leaving half the white pith, and cut to fit the juicer.
- Cut the pineapple to fit the juicer.
- Push the fruit through the juicer using the safety plunger.

Pear and Raspberry Juice

400 g/14 oz pears
100 g/3¹/₂ oz raspberries

- Wash the pears, remove the cores and cut the fruit to fit the juicer.
- Wash the raspberries.
- Push the fruit through the juicer using the safety plunger.

If you find this juice too sweet, try adding a little lemon juice or dilute the juice with apple juice, water or mineral water.

Sweet Pear Surprise

250 g/ 9 oz pears
100 g/3¹/₂ oz orange
125 g/4¹/₂ oz strawberries

- Wash the pears, remove the cores and cut the fruit to fit the juicer.
- Peel the orange, leaving half the white pith, and cut to fit the juicer.
- Wash and hull the strawberries.
- Push the fruit through the juicer using the safety plunger.

Pineapple

Nutrients per 100 g/3¹/₂ oz

Protein	0.4 g
Fat	0.2 g
Carbohydrate	13.7 g
Calcium	17 mg
Phosphorus	8 mg
Magnesium	13 mg
Iron	0.5 mg
Sodium	1 mg
Potassium	146 mg
Vitamin A	70 IU
Vitamin B1	0.09 mg
Viamin B2	0.03 mg
Vitamin B3	0.2 mg
Vitamin C	17 mg
kJ	218
Calories	52

If you've ever had a sore throat and drunk a glass of fresh pineapple juice you will have immediately experienced its valuable soothing and healing properties. It is high in vitamin C, chlorine, potassium, enzymes and fruit acids.

Pineapple juice is particularly high in the enzyme bromelin, which helps the body to balance and neutralise fluids that are either too alkaline or too acidic. Bromelin also has the ability to stimulate hormone secretions in the pancreas. This has made it an invaluable ingredient for the production of certain hormone supplements. The bromelin enzyme has also been associated with the reduction of swelling and inflammation in rheumatoid arthritis, osteoarthritis and gout.

Make sure you choose ripe pineapples for juicing. They should have a yellow skin and sweet smell. To prepare pineapple for juicing, cut thick slices and trim away the skin and the hard core.

Pineapple Juice

400 g/14 oz pineapple
  flesh

- Cut the pineapple to fit the juicer.
- Push the fruit through the juicer using the safety plunger.

Pineapple juice can be diluted ½ part pineapple juice to 1 part water.

Pineapple and Peach Juice

200 g/7 oz pineapple flesh
300 g/10½ oz peaches

- Cut the pineapple to fit the juicer.
- Peel the peaches, remove the stones and cut the fruit to fit the juicer.
- Push the fruit through the juicer using the safety plunger.

Pineapple, Pear and Coconut Juice

200 g/7 oz pineapple
  flesh
150 g/5 oz pears
1 coconut

- Cut the pineapple to fit the juicer.
- Wash the pears, remove the cores and cut the fruit to fit the juicer.
- Open the coconut and measure out 60 ml/ 2 fl oz/¼ cup coconut milk (I use a screwdriver to penetrate the soft eye of the coconut – the coconut milk pours out easily).
- Push the pineapple and pear through the juicer using the safety plunger.
- Add the coconut milk to the fruit juice and stir through.

Raspberry

Nutrients per 100 g/3½ oz

Protein	1.5 g
Fat	1.4 g
Carbohydrate	15.7 g
Calcium	30 mg
Phosphorus	22 mg
Magnesium	30 mg
Iron	0.9 mg
Sodium	1 mg
Potassium	199 mg
Vitamin A	trace
Vitamin B1	0.03 mg
Vitamin B2	0.09 mg
Vitamin B3	0.9 mg
Vitamin C	18 mg
kJ	239
Calories	57

Raspberries are considered by many to be the finest of all the berries. They contain a significant amount of fibre and vitamin C, a moderate amount of magnesium and are high in iron. When juiced, raspberries provide a luscious, thick deep-red purée that is excellent used as a base for other sweet juices.

Raspberry Juice

400 g/14 oz raspberries

- Wash the raspberries.
- Push the raspberries through the juicer using the safety plunger.

Raspberry juice can be diluted 1 part juice to 1–4 parts water.

Raspberry and Apple Juice

100 g/3¹/₂ oz raspberries
300 g/10¹/₂ oz apples

- Wash the raspberries.
- Wash the apples, remove the cores and cut the fruit to fit the juicer.
- Push the fruit through the juicer using the safety plunger.

Raspberry and Pear Juice

100 g/3¹/₂ oz raspberries
400 g/14 oz pears

- Wash the raspberries.
- Wash the pears, remove the cores and cut the fruit to fit the juicer.
- Push the fruit through the juicer using the safety plunger.

Sparkling Raspberry

100 g/3¹/₂ oz raspberries
175 ml/6 fl oz/³/₄ cup
   mineral water

- Wash the raspberries.
- Push the raspberries through the juicer using the safety plunger.
- Add the mineral water and stir through.

Serve over lots of ice garnished with a slice of lemon.

Berry Blush

200 g/7 oz raspberries
200 g/7 oz apricots

- Wash the raspberries.
- Wash the apricots and remove the stones.
- Push the fruit through the juicer using the safety plunger.

Strawberry

Nutrients per 100 g/3½ oz

Protein	0.7 g
Fat	0.5 g
Carbohydrate	8.4 g
Calcium	21 mg
Phosphorus	21 mg
Magnesium	12 mg
Iron	1 mg
Sodium	1 mg
Potassium	164 mg
Vitamin A	60 IU
Vitamin B1	0.03 mg
Viamin B2	0.07 mg
Vitamin B3	0.6 mg
Vitamin C	59 mg
kJ	155
Calories	37

Strawberry juice is rich in vitamin C and minerals such as calcium, phosphorus and potassium. It also contains organic salicylates, which are natural pain-killers and a basic ingredient of aspirin. Its combination of nutrients makes strawberry juice an ideal complexion booster and general tonic for the body. Strawberry juice is sweet and delicious and can be diluted with water or other juices, such as orange, apple or pear.

Make sure your strawberries have not been sprayed. To prepare strawberries for juicing, wash and hull them.

Strawberry Juice

500 g/1 lb 2 oz
strawberries

- Wash and hull the strawberries.
- Push the strawberries through the juicer using the safety plunger.

Strawberry juice can be diluted 1 part strawberry juice to 1–2 parts water. Serve over lots of ice for a really refreshing drink.

Strawberry and Apple Juice

250 g/9 oz strawberries
200 g/7 oz apples

- Wash and hull the strawberries.
- Wash the apples, remove the cores and cut the fruit to fit the juicer.
- Push the fruit through the juicer using the safety plunger.

Strawberry Kiwi Cooler

250 g/9 oz strawberries
350 g/12 oz kiwifruit

- Wash and hull the strawberries.
- Peel the furry skin from the kiwifruit and cut the fruit to fit the juicer.
- Push the fruit through the juicer using the safety plunger.

Strawberry and Peach Juice

250 g/9 oz strawberries
300 g/10½ oz peaches

- Wash and hull the strawberries.
- Peel the peaches and cut the flesh away from the stone.
- Push the fruit through the juicer using the safety plunger.

Strawberry Passion

125 g/4¹/₂ oz strawberries
200 g/7 oz mandarins
2–3 passionfruit

- Wash and hull the strawberries.
- Peel the mandarins and segment to fit the juicer.
- Cut the passionfruit in halves and scoop out the juice and pulp.
- Push the strawberries and mandarin through the juicer using the safety plunger.
- Add the passionfruit juice and pulp to the fruit juice and stir through.

Strawberry Tropics

125 g/4¹/₂ oz strawberries
200 g/7 oz nectarine
* flesh*
150 g/5 oz peach flesh
150 g/5 oz mango flesh

- Wash and hull the strawberries.
- Wash the nectarines and peaches, remove the stones and cut to fit the juicer.
- Push the fruit through the juicer using the safety plunger.

This juice can be transformed into a delicious punch by using 1 part juice to 2 parts mineral water.

Watermelon

Nutrients per 100 g/3½ oz

Protein .... 0.5 g
Fat .... 0.2 g
Carbohydrate ...... 6.4 g
Calcium .... 7 mg
Phosphorus ...... 10 mg
Magnesium .... 8 mg
Iron .... 0.5 mg
Sodium .... 1 mg
Potassium .... 100 mg
Vitamin A .... 590 IU
Vitamin B1 ..... 0.03 mg
Vitamin B2 ..... 0.03 mg
Vitamin B3 .... 0.2 mg
Vitamin C .... 7 mg
kJ 113
Calories 27

Watermelon juice is one of my favourites. Served over lots of crushed ice it is one of the most refreshing summer drinks you are likely to taste. Children love it because of its bright-pink colour, too. Although it tastes sweet, watermelon juice is surprisingly low in kilojoules. It is also rich in vitamin A and potassium. If you juice the rind as well you increase the chlorophyll content of the juice.

Watermelon juice is a natural diuretic and helps flush the kidneys and bladder of excess fluids. It is also high in enzymes and is regarded as an appetite stimulant.

Watermelon Juice

300 g/10¹/₂ oz
  watermelon flesh

- Remove any pips from the watermelon and cut the fruit to fit the juicer.
- Push the watermelon through the juicer using the safety plunger.

Watermelon juice can be diluted 1 part juice to ¹/₂–1 part water.

Watermelon Apple Spice

150 g/5 oz watermelon
  flesh
200 g/7 oz apples
pinch of mixed spice
grated lemon rind

- Remove any pips from the watermelon and cut the fruit to fit the juicer.
- Wash the apples, remove the cores and cut the fruit to fit the juicer.
- Push the fruit through the juicer using the safety plunger.
- Add the mixed spice and lemon rind to taste.

Watermelon Fizz

150 g/5 oz watermelon
125 ml/4 fl oz/¹/₂ cup
  mineral water
mint leaves to garnish

- Remove any pips from the watermelon and cut the fruit to fit the juicer.
- Push the watermelon through the juicer using the safety plunger.
- Add the mineral water and stir through.

Serve over crushed ice and garnish with fresh mint leaves.

Vegetable Juices

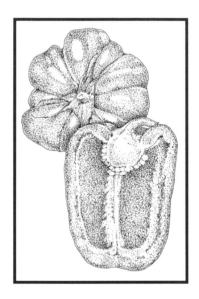

The following recipes for vegetable juices are intended only as a guideline. The combination of vegetable juices will only be limited by your imagination and what you might find in your vegetable crisper at any one time. As you experiment remember to record your successful juice combinations so that you can enjoy them again. (Note that while the tomato is, in fact, a fruit, recipes have been included in this section as the tomato is more usually prepared as a vegetable.)

Vegetable juices contain about half the amount of kilojoules as fruit juices so there is really no restriction on the amount that you can consume. Often referred to as the 'body restorers', vegetable juices are packed with chemical nutrients that restore the blood and provide bone-building minerals. Fresh fruit juices, on the other hand, are known for their body-cleansing potential and their energy life force. Put the two together and you have the makings of one of the finest health and wellbeing programmes available.

Always wash vegetables thoroughly before juicing them to remove any dirt and grit. However, do not wash them in warm or hot water or leave them soaking in water for long periods as this leaches out vital nutrients.

Some vegetable juices, such as beetroot and green juices, are very potent and can upset the digestion system if drunk in large quantities. It is suggested that these juices are diluted with water or cucumber juice or added to other juices in smaller quantities to avoid any discomfort.

The first recipe listed for each vegetable indicates the quantity of that particular vegetable needed to make up a cup (250 ml/8 fl oz) of that juice. When you first begin drinking fresh juices you may find drinking this amount too much or that a particular juice is too potent. Start with a quarter or half the quantity (diluting it if desired) and slowly increase the amount. I have included a suggested dilution ratio you might like to begin with at the end of the first juice recipe for each vegetable. This is only a guideline and can be adjusted to suit your personal taste. Of course, if you are juicing for a family simply multiply the recipe accordingly.

You can enhance the flavour of vegetable juices by adding garlic, fresh ginger, kelp powder (available from health food shops), spices and fresh herbs (such as parsley, basil, oregano, thyme, marjoram, dill, mint, rosemary and sage). Refer to 'Herbs and Spices for Juicing' on page 168 for useful information and tips.

You will find recipes in this section listed under their dominant ingredient (for example, Carrot and Celery Juice appears under 'Carrot').

Asparagus

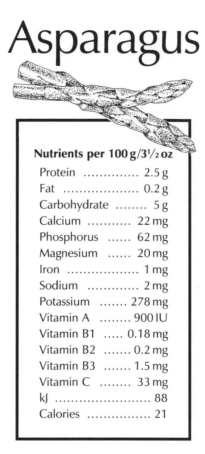

Nutrients per 100 g/3½ oz

Protein .... 2.5 g
Fat .... 0.2 g
Carbohydrate .... 5 g
Calcium .... 22 mg
Phosphorus ...... 62 mg
Magnesium ...... 20 mg
Iron .... 1 mg
Sodium .... 2 mg
Potassium .... 278 mg
Vitamin A .... 900 IU
Vitamin B1 ..... 0.18 mg
Vitamin B2 .... 0.2 mg
Vitamin B3 .... 1.5 mg
Vitamin C .... 33 mg
kJ 88
Calories 21

Asparagus juice is high in vitamins A, B1 and C, choline and potassium. It is a natural and gentle diuretic, is alkaline, reduces the acidity of the blood and cleanses body tissue. It also has a reputation for being able to break down oxalic acid, which contributes to the making of kidney stones.

Asparagus Juice

375 g/13 oz asparagus

- Wash the asparagus.
- Push the asparagus through the juicer using the safety plunger.

Asparagus juice can be diluted 1 part juice to 1–2 parts water.

Asparagus and Beetroot Juice

125 g/4¹/₂ oz asparagus
100 g/3¹/₂ oz beetroot
125 ml/4 fl oz/¹/₂ cup
water

- Wash the asparagus.
- Wash the beetroot and cut to fit the juicer.
- Push the vegetables through the juicer using the safety plunger.
- Add water to the juice and stir through.

For a taste variation juice 200 g/7 oz cucumber instead of adding the water.

Asparagus and Carrot Juice

125 g/4¹/₂ oz asparagus
300 g/10¹/₂ oz carrots

- Wash the asparagus.
- Wash the carrots and cut to fit the juicer.
- Push the vegetables through the juicer using the safety plunger.

Asparagus and Cucumber Juice

125 g/4¹/₂ oz asparagus
250 g/ 9 oz cucumber

- Wash the asparagus.
- Peel the cucumber and cut to fit the juicer.
- Push the vegetables through the juicer using the safety plunger.

Green Forest Juice

100 g/3¹/₂ oz asparagus
50 g/ 2 oz lettuce
50 g/ 2 oz spinach
100 g/3¹/₂ oz celery
50 g/ 2 oz alfalfa sprouts
50 g/ 2 oz green capsicum

- Wash the asparagus.
- Wash the lettuce and spinach thoroughly and shake dry.
- Wash the celery. Do not remove the foliage.
- Wash the capsicum, remove the seeds and cut to fit the juicer.
- Push the vegetables through the juicer using the safety plunger.

Bean

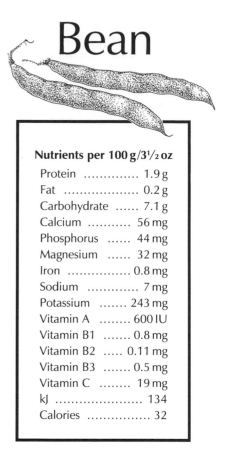

Nutrients per 100 g/3½ oz

Protein .... 1.9 g
Fat .... 0.2 g
Carbohydrate ...... 7.1 g
Calcium .... 56 mg
Phosphorus ...... 44 mg
Magnesium ...... 32 mg
Iron .... 0.8 mg
Sodium .... 7 mg
Potassium .... 243 mg
Vitamin A .... 600 IU
Vitamin B1 .... 0.8 mg
Vitamin B2 ..... 0.11 mg
Vitamin B3 .... 0.5 mg
Vitamin C .... 19 mg
kJ 134
Calories 32

Bean juice is rich in B group vitamins, calcium, magnesium, phosphorus, potassium, protein and sulphur. It also contains elements that assist the pancreas to produce natural insulin, is a body cleanser, is recommended for conditions of anaemia, diabetes and hypoglycaemia and aids weight loss.

Bean Juice

400 g/14 oz beans

- Wash the beans.
- Push the beans through the juicer using the safety plunger.

Bean juice can be diluted 1 part juice to 1 part water.

Bean, Apple and Celery Juice

100 g/3¹/₂ oz beans
200 g/7 oz apples
100 g/3¹/₂ oz celery

- Wash the beans.
- Wash the apples, remove the cores and cut the fruit to fit the juicer.
- Wash the celery. Do not remove the foliage.
- Push the beans, apple and celery through the juicer using the safety plunger.

Try adding some finely chopped fresh herbs, such as mint, thyme, oregano or basil, to this tasty drink.

Bean, Capsicum and Carrot Juice

100 g/3¹/₂ oz beans
100 g/3¹/₂ oz capsicum
200 g/7 oz carrots

- Wash the beans.
- Wash the capsicum, remove the seeds and cut to fit the juicer.
- Wash the carrots and cut to fit the juicer.
- Push the vegetables through the juicer using the safety plunger.

Beetroot

Nutrients per 100 g/3½ oz

Protein .... 1.6 g
Fat .... 0.1 g
Carbohydrate ...... 9.9 g
Calcium .... 16 mg
Phosphorus ...... 33 mg
Magnesium ...... 25 mg
Iron .... 0.7 mg
Sodium .... 60 mg
Potassium .... 335 mg
Vitamin A .... 20 IU
Vitamin B1 ..... 0.03 mg
Vitamin B2 ..... 0.05 mg
Vitamin B3 .... 0.4 mg
Vitamin C .... 10 mg
kJ 167
Calories 40

Beetroot juice is probably one of the most powerful cleansing and blood-building juices available. It contains four of the most important vitamins and nine of the essential minerals while also having a high natural sugar content. In addition, it has small amounts of very good quality iron to build red blood.

Beetroot juice has been used in the treatment of kidney and bladder disorders, gallstones, jaundice, gout, constipation, anaemia, menstrual problems and cancer.

For the best flavour, juice the small, young beetroot. If you juice the beet tops you will get a good amount of chlorophyll, vitamins A and C, calcium and potassium too.

The juice is ruby-red in colour. It has a strong taste and because of its powerful kidney and blood-cleansing properties, it is best to drink it in moderation or diluted.

Beetroot Juice

400 g/14 oz beetroot

- Wash the beetroot and cut to fit the juicer.
- Push the beetroot through the juicer using the safety plunger.

Beetroot juice can be diluted 1 part juice to 1–4 parts water.

Beetroot, Apple and Celery Juice

100 g/3¹/₂ oz beetroot
200 g/7 oz apples
100 g/3¹/₂ oz celery

- Wash the beetroot and cut to fit the juicer.
- Wash the apples, remove the cores and cut the fruit to fit the juicer.
- Wash the celery. Do not remove the foliage.
- Push the beetroot, apple and celery through the juicer using the safety plunger.

Beetroot, Carrot and Celery Juice

100 g/3¹/₂ oz beetroot
200 g/7 oz carrots
100 g/3¹/₂ oz celery

- Wash the beetroot and carrots and cut to fit the juicer.
- Wash the celery. Do not remove the foliage.
- Push the beetroot, carrot and celery through the juicer using the safety plunger.

Beetroot, Cucumber, Apple and Carrot Juice

50 g/ 2 oz beetroot
50 g/ 2 oz cucumber
200 g/ 7 oz apples
100 g/3¹/₂ oz carrot

- Wash the beetroot and cut to fit the juicer.
- Peel the cucumber and cut to fit the juicer.
- Wash the apples, remove the cores and cut the fruit to fit the juicer.
- Wash the carrot and cut to fit the juicer.
- Push the beetroot, cucumber, apple and carrot through the juicer using the safety plunger.

Beetroot, Pineapple and Cucumber Juice

100 g/3¹/₂ oz beetroot
100 g/3¹/₂ oz pineapple
flesh
150 g/5 oz cucumber

- Wash the beetroot and cut to fit the juicer.
- Cut the pineapple to fit the juicer.
- Peel the cucumber and cut to fit the juicer.
- Push the beetroot, pineapple and cucumber through the juicer using the safety plunger.

See colour plate opposite page 75.

Broccoli

Nutrients per 100 g/3¹/₂ oz

Protein .... 3.6 g

Fat .... 0.3 g

Carbohydrate ...... 5.9 g

Calcium .... 103 mg

Phosphorus ...... 78 mg

Magnesium ...... 24 mg

Iron .... 1.1 mg

Sodium .... 15 mg

Potassium .... 382 mg

Vitamin A ...... 2500 IU

Vitamin B1 .... 0.1 mg

Vitamin B2 ..... 0.23 mg

Vitamin B3 .... 0.9 mg

Vitamin C .... 113 mg

kJ 147

Calories 35

Fresh broccoli juice contains two-thirds more vitamin C than cooked broccoli, as well as good amounts of vitamin A and calcium, and is best diluted or combined with other juices.

Choose bright-green, compact heads of broccoli with tender stalks for the best juice. Do not juice any broccoli that has begun to turn yellow or that has very woody stems. While you can juice all the broccoli you may prefer to remove the small green leaves, which sometimes produce a bitter taste.

Broccoli Juice

800 g/1 lb 2 oz broccoli

- Wash the broccoli and break into florets to fit the juicer.
- Push the broccoli through the juicer using the safety plunger.

Broccoli juice can be diluted 1 part juice to 1–3 parts water.

Broccoli, Carrot and Cucumber Juice

200 g/7 oz broccoli
200 g/7 oz carrots
100 g/3¹/₂ oz cucumber

- Wash the broccoli and break into florets to fit the juicer.
- Wash the carrots and cut to fit the juicer.
- Peel the cucumber and cut to fit the juicer.
- Push the vegetables through the juicer using the safety plunger.

Broccoli, Carrot, Tomato and Spinach Juice

200 g/7 oz broccoli
150 g/5 oz carrots
100 g/3¹/₂ oz tomato
50 g/2 oz spinach

- Wash the broccoli and break into florets to fit the juicer.
- Wash the carrots and tomato and cut to fit the juicer.
- Wash the spinach.
- Push the broccoli, carrot, tomato and spinach through the juicer using the safety plunger.

Broccoli, Celery, Tomato, Capsicum and Garlic Juice

200 g/ 7 oz broccoli
100 g/3¹/₂ oz celery
100 g/3¹/₂ oz tomato
100 g/3¹/₂ oz capsicum
2 cloves garlic

- Wash the broccoli and break into florets to fit the juicer.
- Wash the celery. Do not remove the foliage.
- Wash the tomato and cut to fit the juicer.
- Wash the capsicum, remove the seeds and cut to fit the juicer.
- Peel the garlic.
- Push the broccoli, celery, tomato, capsicum and garlic through the juicer using the safety plunger.

Cabbage

Nutrients per 100 g/3¹/₂ oz

Protein .... 2.4 g
Fat .... 0.2 g
Carbohydrate ...... 4.6 g
Calcium .... 67 mg
Phosphorus ...... 54 mg
Magnesium .... —
Iron .... 0.9 mg
Sodium .... 22 mg
Potassium .... 269 mg
Vitamin A .... 200 IU
Vitamin B1 ..... 0.05 mg
Vitamin B2 ..... 0.08 mg
Vitamin B3 .... 0.3 mg
Vitamin C .... 55 mg
kJ 101
Calories 24

Cabbage juice is probably my least favourite juice but it is worth holding your nose as it goes down because of its nutrient makeup. The strong smell comes from its high sulphur content. It is also high in chlorine and calcium and has smaller amounts of iodine. In addition, cabbage juice provides a valuable source of vitamins A and B, and some potassium, iron and a little vitamin C. Mix all these things together and you have a very powerful body-cleansing tonic. Cabbage juice comes highly recommended for people wanting to lose weight, alleviate constipation or improve poor skin. The vitamin U in cabbage is said to have healing properties beneficial for intestinal ulcers.

Because of its strong taste it is best to dilute cabbage juice with water or other suitable juices, such as carrot, cucumber, tomato and green juices. Undiluted it can cause gas and cramping in the intestine for some people.

Cabbage Juice

400 g/14 oz cabbage

- Wash the cabbage and cut to fit the juicer.
- Push the cabbage through the juicer using the safety plunger.

Cabbage juice can be diluted 1 part juice to 1–3 parts water.

Cabbage and Carrot Juice

100 g/3¹/₂ oz cabbage
300 g/10¹/₂ oz carrots

- Wash the cabbage and carrots and cut to fit the juicer.
- Push the vegetables through the juicer using the safety plunger.

Cabbage, Celery and Fennel Juice

100 g/3¹/₂ oz cabbage
200 g/7 oz celery
100 g/3¹/₂ oz fennel

- Wash the cabbage and cut to fit the juicer.
- Wash the celery. Do not remove the foliage.
- Wash the fennel and cut to fit the juicer.
- Push the vegetables through the juicer using the safety plunger.

Cabbage Patch

100 g/3¹/₂ oz cabbage
100 g/3¹/₂ oz carrots
100 g/3¹/₂ oz tomato
100 g/3¹/₂ oz cucumber

- Wash the cabbage, carrots and tomato and cut to fit the juicer.
- Peel the cucumber and cut to fit the juicer.
- Push the cabbage, carrot, tomato and cucumber through the juicer using the safety plunger.

Cabbage, Lettuce, Celery, Spinach and Carrot Juice

100 g/3¹/₂ oz cabbage
100 /3¹/₂ oz lettuce
50 g/2 oz celery
50 g/2 oz spinach
100 g/3¹/₂ oz carrots

- Wash the cabbage and lettuce and cut to fit the juicer.
- Wash the celery. Do not remove the foliage.
- Wash the spinach.
- Wash the carrots and cut to fit the juicer
- Push the vegetables through the juicer using the safety plunger.

Capsicum

Nutrients per 100 g/3½ oz

	Green	Red
Protein	1.2 g	1.4 g
Fat	0.2 g	0.3 g
Carbohydrate	4.8 g	7.1 g
Calcium	9 mg	13 mg
Phosphorus	22 mg	30 mg
Magnesium	18 mg	18 mg
Iron	0.7 mg	0.6 mg
Sodium	13 mg	13 mg
Potassium	213 mg	213 mg
Vitamin A	420 IU	4450 IU
Vitamin B1	0.08 mg	0.08 mg
Vitamin B2	0.08 mg	0.08 mg
Vitamin B3	0.5 mg	0.5 mg
Vitamin C	128 mg	204 mg
kJ	92	92
Calories	22	22

Both green and red capsicum are rich in nutrients such as potassium and silicon and high in Vitamin C. Ripe, red capsicum are especially high in Vitamin A. Capsicum juice is excellent for stimulating blood circulation as it tones and cleanses the arteries. Capsicum juice is a vibrant colour and tastes delicately sweet and slightly peppery. Always remove the seeds before juicing capsicum as they can be bitter and hot.

Capsicum Juice

400 g/14 oz capsicum

- Wash the capsicum, remove the seeds and cut to fit the juicer.
- Push the capsicum through the juicer using the safety plunger.

Capsicum juice can be diluted 1 part juice to ½–1 part water.

Capsicum, Celery and Spinach Juice

200 g/7 oz red capsicum
100 g/3½ oz cucumber
50 g/2 oz celery
50 g/2 oz spinach

- Wash the capsicum, remove the seeds and cut to fit the juicer.
- Peel the cucumber and cut to fit the juicer.
- Wash the celery. Do not remove the foliage.
- Wash the spinach.
- Push the vegetables through the juicer using the safety plunger.

Capsicum, Cucumber, Garlic and Basil Juice

100 g/3½ oz red
  capsicum
100 g/3½ oz green
  capsicum
100 g/3½ oz cucumber
2 cloves garlic
small handful of fresh
  basil

- Wash the capsicum, remove the seeds and cut to fit the juicer.
- Peel the cucumber and cut to fit the juicer.
- Peel the garlic.
- Push the vegetables and basil through the juicer using the safety plunger.

OPPOSITE: Tomato Juice (page 146) and Lettuce and Greens Cocktail (page 136).

Capsi-Italiano

90 g/3 oz red capsicum
90 g/3 oz green capsicum
100 g/3½ oz tomato
100 g/3½ oz carrot
1–2 cloves garlic
small handful of fresh
basil

- Wash the capsicum, remove the seeds and cut to fit the juicer.
- Wash the tomato and cut to fit the juicer.
- Wash the carrot and cut to fit the juicer.
- Peel the garlic.
- Push the tomato, carrot, capsicum, garlic and basil through the juicer using the safety plunger.

Peppery Tonic

100 g/3½ oz green
capsicum
100 g/3½ oz red
capsicum
150 g/5 oz carrots
cayenne pepper to taste

- Wash the capsicum, remove the seeds and cut to fit the juicer.
- Wash the carrots and cut to fit the juicer.
- Push the vegetables through the juicer using the safety plunger.
- Add cayenne pepper to taste.

OPPOSITE: Cream of Avocado Soup (page 152) and Carrot, Tomato and Basil Soup (page 153).

Carrot

Nutrients per 100 g/3½ oz

Protein	1.1 g
Fat	0.2 g
Carbohydrate	9.7 g
Calcium	37 mg
Phosphorus	36 mg
Magnesium	23 mg
Iron	0.7 mg
Sodium	47 mg
Potassium	341 mg
Vitamin A	11 000 IU
Vitamin B1	0.06 mg
Vitamin B2	0.05 mg
Vitamin B3	0.6 mg
Vitamin C	8 mg
kJ	151
Calories	36

Carrot juice is undoubtedly the most popular of the vegetable juices. It is delicious on its own and mixes well with all other vegetable juices and a number of fruit juices.

The beta-carotene in carrots (vitamin A) is an important anti-cancer agent and helps to fight infections. Carrot juice is also high in potassium, sodium, calcium and magnesium, which makes it alkaline in nature. It is regarded as a digestion stimulant, a mild diuretic and a liver cleanser; it also helps to break down excess fats and cholesterol in the liver. Like string beans, carrots contain an insulin-like compound, so they are highly recommended for diabetics.

Many people believe too much carrot juice is toxic. This is not the case. It is true that vitamin A as retinol in a pre-formed state could produce toxic effects if given in large doses over a period of time. However, beta-carotene, the main pro-vitamin A in vegetables, appears to be non-toxic. Should your skin begin turning yellow when you drink carrot juice, it means that the liver is excreting a build-up of toxic wastes. In this case, dilute your carrot juice with water or other juices. But, whatever you do, don't stop drinking carrot juice – you'll just miss out on all the wonderful health benefits it provides!

Carrot Juice

400 g/14 oz carrots

- Wash the carrots and cut to fit the juicer.
- Push the carrots through the juicer using the safety plunger.

Carrot juice can be diluted 1 part juice to 1 part water.

Carrot and Alfalfa Juice

200 g/7 oz carrots
200 g/7 oz alfalfa sprouts

- Wash the carrots and cut to fit the juicer.
- Push the alfalfa sprouts and carrot through the juicer using the safety plunger.

Carrot, Capsicum, Celery and Garlic Juice

200 g/7 oz carrots
100 g/3¹/₂ oz red capsicum
100 g/3¹/₂ oz celery
2 cloves garlic

- Wash the carrots and cut to fit the juicer.
- Wash the capsicum, remove the seeds and cut to fit the juicer.
- Wash the celery. Do not remove the foliage.
- Peel the garlic.
- Push the carrot, capsicum, celery and garlic through the juicer using the safety plunger.

Carrot and Celery Juice

200 g/ 7 oz carrots
200 g/ 7 oz celery

- Wash the carrots and cut to fit the juicer.
- Wash the celery. Do not remove the foliage.
- Push the vegetables through the juicer using the safety plunger.

Carrot, Cucumber and Ginger Juice

200 / 7 oz carrots
200 g/ 7 oz cucumber
2.5 cm/1 inch piece
  ginger

- Wash the carrots and cut to fit the juicer.
- Peel the cucumber and cut to fit the juicer.
- Peel the ginger.
- Push the carrot, cucumber and ginger through the juicer using the safety plunger.

See colour plate opposite page 75.

Carrot, Orange and Ginger Juice

200 g/ 7 oz carrots
200 g/ 7 oz oranges
2.5 cm/1 inch piece
  ginger

- Wash the carrots and cut to fit the juicer.
- Peel the oranges, leaving half the white pith, and cut to fit the juicer.
- Peel the ginger.
- Push the carrot, orange and ginger through the juicer using the safety plunger.

Carrot and Parsnip Juice

200 g/ 7 oz carrots
400 g/14 oz parsnips

- Wash the carrots and parsnips and cut to fit the juicer.
- Push the vegetables through the juicer using the safety plunger.

This juice is especially delicious when finely grated lemon and orange rind or finely chopped fresh oregano or dill is added to it.

Carrot, Spinach and Parsley Juice

300 g/10¹/₂ oz carrots
50 g/2 oz spinach
50 g/2 oz parsley

- Wash the carrots and cut to fit the juicer.
- Wash the spinach and parsley.
- Push the carrot, spinach and parsley through the juicer using the safety plunger.

Carrot, Tomato and Beetroot Juice

200 g/7 oz carrots
150 g/5 oz tomatoes
50 g/2 oz beetroot

- Wash the carrots and cut to fit the juicer.
- Wash the tomatoes and cut to fit the juicer.
- Wash the beetroot and cut to fit the juicer.
- Push the carrot, tomato and beetroot through the juicer using the safety plunger.

Try serving this juice with a dash of cayenne pepper or some finely chopped fresh basil.

Cauliflower

Nutrients per 100 g/3¹/₂ oz

Protein .... 2.7 g
Fat .... 0.2 g
Carbohydrate ...... 5.2 g
Calcium .... 25 mg
Phosphorus ...... 56 mg
Magnesium ...... 24 mg
Iron .... 1.1 mg
Sodium .... 13 mg
Potassium .... 295 mg
Vitamin A .... 60 IU
Vitamin B1 ..... 0.11 mg
Vitamin B2 .... 0.1 mg
Vitamin B3 .... 0.7 mg
Vitamin C .... 78 mg
kJ 109
Calories 26

Cauliflower is a member of the cabbage family and is sought after for its cancer-preventing enzymes. The juice is full of vitamin C and the B group vitamins, as well as potassium and some vitamin K. Like mushrooms, cauliflower is recommended for vegetarians.

Look for cauliflowers with white or cream, tightly packed heads. Cauliflower juice is not the most palatable juice on its own but it mixes well with most other vegetable juices.

Cauliflower Juice

800 g/1 lb 12 oz
cauliflower

- Wash the cauliflower and break into florets to fit the juicer.
- Push the cauliflower through the juicer using the safety plunger.

Cauliflower juice can be diluted 1 part juice to 2–3 parts water.

Cauliflower, Carrot and Tomato Juice

200 g/7 oz cauliflower
200 g/7 oz carrots
100 g/3¹/₂ oz tomato

- Wash the cauliflower and break into florets to fit the juicer.
- Wash the carrots and tomato and cut to fit the juicer.
- Push the cauliflower, carrot and tomato through the juicer using the safety plunger.

Cauliflower, Cucumber and Apple Juice

200 g/7 oz cauliflower
100 g/3¹/₂ oz cucumber
200 g/7 oz apples

- Wash the cauliflower and break into florets to fit the juicer.
- Peel the cucumber and cut to fit the juicer.
- Wash the apples, remove the cores and cut the fruit to fit the juicer.
- Push the cauliflower, cucumber and apple through the juicer using the safety plunger.

Celery

Nutrients per 100 g/3½ oz

Protein .... 0.9 g
Fat .... 0.1 g
Carbohydrate ...... 3.9 g
Calcium .... 39 mg
Phosphorus ...... 28 mg
Magnesium ...... 22 mg
Iron .... 0.3 mg
Sodium .... 126 mg
Potassium .... 341 mg
Vitamin A .... 240 IU
Vitamin B1 ..... 0.03 mg
Vitamin B2 ..... 0.03 mg
Vitamin B3 .... 0.3 mg
Vitamin C .... 9 mg
kJ 75
Calories 18

Celery has one of the highest amounts of organic sodium found in vegetables suitable for juicing. Organic sodium is needed by all major body systems to carry out effective body functions, and is also responsible for maintaining body fluids, vitamin C and potassium in the body. Along with other minerals that are largely alkaline, the high levels of organic sodium make celery an excellent stress-reducing or calming juice. Celery also contains minerals that help effective utilisation of calcium. Because of its high amounts of magnesium and iron celery is said to be good for building blood cells. It is also recommended in weight-loss programmes. Like cucumber juice, celery juice is a natural diuretic and helps to cleanse and flush the body of toxic wastes.

Juice the whole celery stick, including the green leaves, which are a major source of chlorophyll. Do not juice soft or wilting celery – the celery sticks should be a bright vivid green and snap crisply.

Celery Juice

400 g/14 oz celery

- Wash the celery. Do not remove the foliage.
- Push the celery through the juicer using the safety plunger.

Celery juice can be diluted 1 part juice to 1 part water.

Celery, Asparagus, Carrot and Tomato Juice

200 g/7 oz celery
50 g/2 oz asparagus
100 g/3¹/₂ oz carrots
50 g/2 oz tomato

- Wash the celery. Do not remove the foliage.
- Wash the asparagus.
- Wash the carrots and tomato and cut to fit the juicer.
- Push the celery, asparagus, carrot and tomato through the juicer using the safety plunger.

Celery, Beetroot and Alfalfa Juice

100 g/3¹/₂ oz celery
50 g/2 oz beetroot
200 g/7 oz alfalfa
  sprouts

- Wash the celery. Do not remove the foliage.
- Wash the beetroot and cut to fit the juicer.
- Push the alfalfa sprouts, celery and beetroot through the juicer using the safety plunger.

Add some finely chopped fresh parsley to the juice for extra flavour.

Celery, Cabbage and Fennel Juice

250 g/9 oz celery
100 g/3¹/₂ oz cabbage
50 g/2 oz fennel

- Wash the celery. Do not remove the foliage.
- Wash the cabbage and fennel and cut to fit the juicer.
- Push the vegetables through the juicer using the safety plunger.

Celery and Cucumber Juice

200 g/7 oz celery
200 g/7 oz cucumber

- Wash the celery. Do not remove the foliage.
- Peel the cucumber and cut to fit the juicer.
- Push the celery and cucumber through the juicer using the safety plunger.

Celery, Spinach and Apple Juice

200 g/7 oz celery
50 g/2 oz spinach
150 g/5 oz apples

- Wash the celery. Do not remove the foliage.
- Wash the spinach.
- Wash the apples, remove the cores and cut the fruit to fit the juicer.
- Push the celery, spinach and apple through the juicer using the safety plunger.

Cucumber

Nutrients per 100 g/3½ oz

Protein	0.9 g
Fat	0.1 g
Carbohydrate	3.4 g
Calcium	25 mg
Phosphorus	27 mg
Magnesium	11 mg
Iron	1.1 mg
Sodium	6 mg
Potassium	160 mg
Vitamin A	250 IU
Vitamin B1	0.03 mg
Vitamin B2	0.04 mg
Vitamin B3	0.2 mg
Vitamin C	11 mg
kJ	59
Calories	14

Cucumber juice is by far the best natural diuretic known. Cucumbers are comprised largely of water, which helps to eliminate toxic wastes and excess fluid through urine flow. They are high in potassium, sodium, phosphorus and chlorine.

The organic ingredients of cucumbers are said to dissolve kidney stones, cleanse and rejuvenate the skin and reduce blood pressure. The silicon, sulphur and trace elements found in cucumber juice are also great for healthy hair and nails.

If you grow your own cucumbers you can leave the peel on when juicing them. You will find good amounts of vitamin A in the skin. Most commercially grown cucumbers, however, tend to be waxed and it is best to peel them before juicing. You can add vitamin A to the juice simply by adding a carrot or two.

Look for dark-green, firm-skinned cucumbers without blemishes or soft spots. These will yield the most juice with the best flavour.

Cucumber Juice

400 g/14 oz cucumber

- Peel the cucumber and cut to fit the juicer.
- Push the cucumber through the juicer using the safety plunger.

Cucumber juice is a relatively bland juice and it is best in its undiluted state.

Cucumber and Apple Juice

200 g/7 oz cucumber
200 g/7 oz apples

- Peel the cucumber and cut to fit the juicer.
- Wash the apples, remove the cores and cut the fruit to fit the juicer.
- Push the cucumber and apple through the juicer using the safety plunger.

Cucumber and Carrot Juice

200 g/7 oz cucumber
200 g/7 oz carrots

- Peel the cucumber and cut to fit the juicer.
- Wash the carrots and cut to fit the juicer.
- Push the cucumber and carrot through the juicer using the safety plunger.

Cucumber and Pineapple Juice

200 g/7 oz cucumber
200 g/7 oz pineapple
  flesh

- Peel the cucumber and cut to fit the juicer.
- Cut the pineapple to fit the juicer.
- Push the cucumber and pineapple through the juicer using the safety plunger.

Lettuce

Nutrients per 100 g/3½ oz	
Protein	1.3 g
Fat	0.3 g
Carbohydrate	3.5 g
Calcium	68 mg
Phosphorus	25 mg
Magnesium	—
Iron	1.4 mg
Sodium	9 mg
Potassium	264 mg
Vitamin A	1900 IU
Vitamin B1	0.05 mg
Vitamin B2	0.08 mg
Vitamin B3	0.4 mg
Vitamin C	18 mg
kJ	59
Calories	14

Choose dark-green lettuce for juicing as these have higher levels of calcium, chlorophyll, iron, potassium, silicon and vitamins A and E. Lettuce juice is a natural body cleanser and body builder and is best combined with other juices, such as celery and carrot or green juices.

Lettuce Juice

400 g/14 oz lettuce

- Wash the lettuce.
- Push the lettuce through the juicer using the safety plunger.

Lettuce juice can be diluted 1 part juice to 1–2 parts water.

Lettuce and Fennel Juice

300 g/10¹/₂ oz lettuce
100 g/3¹/₂ oz fennel

- Wash the lettuce.
- Wash the fennel and cut to fit the juicer.
- Push the vegetables through the juicer using the safety plunger.

Lettuce and Greens Cocktail

50 g/2 oz lettuce
50 g/2 oz spinach
50 g/2 oz wheatgrass
50 g/2 oz celery
50 g/2 oz cucumber
50 g/2 oz green
   capsicum

- Wash the lettuce, spinach and wheatgrass.
- Wash the celery. Do not remove the foliage.
- Peel the cucumber and cut to fit the juicer.
- Wash the capsicum, remove the seeds and cut to fit the juicer.
- Push the vegetables through the juicer using the safety plunger.

See colour plate opposite page 122.

Mushroom

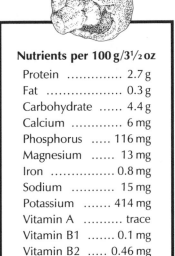

Nutrients per 100 g/3½ oz	
Protein	2.7 g
Fat	0.3 g
Carbohydrate	4.4 g
Calcium	6 mg
Phosphorus	116 mg
Magnesium	13 mg
Iron	0.8 mg
Sodium	15 mg
Potassium	414 mg
Vitamin A	trace
Vitamin B1	0.1 mg
Vitamin B2	0.46 mg
Vitamin B3	4.2 mg
Vitamin C	3 mg
kJ	92
Calories	22

Mushrooms are an excellent source of the B group of vitamins (especially B12, which is essential in a vegetarian diet), iron and potassium. Mushroom juice, while too strong to drink undiluted, combines well with tomato, apple or celery juice. For extra flavour add fresh herbs, such as parsley or dill. Buy the mushrooms fresh and store in the refrigerator in a brown paper bag.

Mushroom Juice

400 g/14 oz mushrooms
- Wash the mushrooms and pat them dry.
- Push the mushrooms through the juicer using the safety plunger.

Add small quantities to other juices or dilute it 1 part juice to 4–6 parts water.

Onion

Nutrients per 100 g/3½ oz

Protein .... 1.5 g
Fat .... 0.1 g
Carbohydrate ...... 8.7 g
Calcium .... 27 mg
Phosphorus ...... 36 mg
Magnesium ...... 12 mg
Iron .... 0.5 mg
Sodium .... 10 mg
Potassium .... 157 mg
Vitamin A .... 40 IU
Vitamin B1 ..... 0.03 mg
Vitamin B2 ..... 0.04 mg
Vitamin B3 .... 0.2 mg
Vitamin C .... 10 mg
kJ 147
Calories 35

Undiluted onion juice is probably too pungent for most people. But with the addition of a little honey it is an ideal juice for treating coughs, colds and for breaking up mucus in the lungs, sinuses and digestive tract.

Onion Juice

400 g/14 oz onions

- Peel the onions and cut to fit the juicer.
- Push the onion through the juicer using the safety plunger.

Onion juice can be diluted 1 part juice to 1–4 parts water.

OPPOSITE: Jamaican Dream (page 159) and Summer Bliss (page 161).

Onion and Honey Juice

400 g/14 oz onions
1 teaspoon honey

- Peel the onions and cut to fit the juicer.
- Push the onion through the juicer using the safety plunger.
- Stir the honey through the juice.

Onion Surprise

50 g/2 oz onion
150 g/5 oz carrots
100 g/3¹/₂ oz tomato
100 g/3¹/₂ oz celery

- Peel the onion and cut to fit the juicer.
- Wash the carrots and tomato and cut to fit the juicer.
- Wash the celery. Do not remove the foliage.
- Push the onion, carrot, tomato and celery through the juicer using the safety plunger.

OPPOSITE: *Kiwi Islander Sorbet (page 165) and Orange and Passionfruit Sorbet (page 166).*

Parsnip

Nutrients per 100 g/3½ oz

Protein	1.7 g
Fat	0.5 g
Carbohydrate	17.5 g
Calcium	50 mg
Phosphorus	77 mg
Magnesium	32 mg
Iron	0.7 mg
Sodium	12 mg
Potassium	541 mg
Vitamin A	30 IU
Vitamin B1	0.07 mg
Vitamin B2	0.08 mg
Vitamin B3	0.1 mg
Vitamin C	10 mg
kJ	293
Calories	70

I have never quite forgotten my first experience of wonderfully sweet mashed parsnip and carrot, which became a favourite vegetable dish of my childhood. By combining the delicious flavours of parsnip and carrot juice I can almost believe I am partaking of this treat all over again.

Parsnip juice by itself is a creamy coloured sweet juice that is a good source of vitamin C, chlorine, phosphorus, potassium, silicon and sulphur. It is recommended as a general tonic and especially for healthy skin, hair and nails.

Parsnip Juice

800 g/1 lb 12 oz
parsnips

- Wash the parsnips and cut to fit the juicer.
- Push the parsnip through the juicer using the safety plunger.

Parsnip juice can be diluted 1 part juice to 1–4 parts water.

Parsnip and Carrot Juice

400 g/14 oz parsnips
200 g/7 oz carrots

- Wash the parsnips and carrots and cut to fit the juicer.
- Push the vegetables through the juicer using the safety plunger.

Parsnip and Greens

400 g/14 oz parsnips
50 g/2 oz cucumber
50 g/2 oz lettuce
50 g/2 oz spinach
50 g/2 oz alfalfa sprouts

- Wash the parsnips and cut to fit the juicer.
- Peel the cucumber and cut to fit the juicer.
- Wash the lettuce and spinach.
- Push the vegetables, including the alfalfa, through the juicer using the safety plunger.

Potato

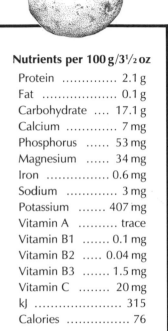

Nutrients per 100 g/3½ oz

Protein .... 2.1 g
Fat .... 0.1 g
Carbohydrate .... 17.1 g
Calcium .... 7 mg
Phosphorus ...... 53 mg
Magnesium ...... 34 mg
Iron .... 0.6 mg
Sodium .... 3 mg
Potassium .... 407 mg
Vitamin A .... trace
Vitamin B1 .... 0.1 mg
Vitamin B2 ..... 0.04 mg
Vitamin B3 .... 1.5 mg
Vitamin C .... 20 mg
kJ 315
Calories 76

Potato juice, while not palatable on its own, is highly nutritious and adds vitamins B and C, calcium, iron and carbohydrate value to juices such as carrot, watercress and tomato.

Potato Juice

400 g/14 oz potatoes

- Peel the potatoes and cut to fit the juicer.
- Push the potatoes through the juicer using the safety plunger.

Potato juice can be diluted 1 part juice to 1–2 parts water.

Spinach

Nutrients per 100 g/3½ oz

Protein .... 3.2 g
Fat .... 0.3 g
Carbohydrate ...... 4.3 g
Calcium .... 93 mg
Phosphorus ...... 51 mg
Magnesium ...... 88 mg
Iron .... 3.1 mg
Sodium .... 71 mg
Potassium .... 470 mg
Vitamin A ...... 8100 IU
Vitamin B1 .... 0.1 mg
Vitamin B2 .... 0.2 mg
Vitamin B3 .... 0.6 mg
Vitamin C .... 51 mg
kJ 96
Calories 23

As an avid fan of the Popeye cartoon I grew up in an age believing that if you ate spinach you could do almost anything. And when you look at its nutritional properties it's not hard to see why this is likely to be true. As a juice it is an excellent source of chlorophyll and vitamin A. It is rich in iron and a good source of iodine, B complex vitamins, calcium, magnesium, phosphorus, potassium, sodium and trace elements.

Spinach juice has a mild laxative effect. It not only cleanses but also helps to reconstruct and regenerate the whole of the digestive tract, including the large intestine. Its organic properties stimulate and tone the liver and gall bladder and aid blood and lymph circulation. The properties of spinach are mainly alkaline so it is especially good for strengthening teeth and gums.

It is important to note, however, that spinach juice is high in oxalic acid, so it should be drunk in small quantities and preferrably diluted with water or other juices.

When buying spinach look for fresh, bright-green leaves. Avoid wilted, overly moist or yellow leaves. Always wash spinach leaves thoroughly to remove sand and dirt and shake dry before juicing.

Spinach Juice

400 g/14 oz spinach

- Wash the spinach.
- Push the spinach through the juicer using the safety plunger.

Spinach juice can be diluted 1 part juice to 2–4 parts water.

Spinach, Apple and Cucumber Juice

100 g/3½ oz spinach
200 g/7 oz apples
100 g/3½ oz cucumber

- Wash the spinach.
- Wash the apples, remove the cores and cut the fruit to fit the juicer.
- Peel the cucumber and cut to fit the juicer.
- Push the spinach, apple and cucumber through the juicer using the safety plunger.

Popeye's Energy Cocktail

50 g/2 oz spinach
200 g/7 oz carrots
100 g/3½ oz cucumber
50 g/2 oz celery
2 cloves garlic

- Wash the spinach.
- Wash the carrots and cut to fit the juicer.
- Peel the cucumber and cut to fit the juicer.
- Wash the celery. Do not remove the foliage.
- Peel the garlic.
- Push the vegetables through the juicer using the safety plunger.

Tomato

Nutrients per 100 g/3¹/₂ oz

Protein .... 1.1 g
Fat .... 0.2 g
Carbohydrate ...... 4.7 g
Calcium .... 13 mg
Phosphorus ...... 27 mg
Magnesium ...... 14 mg
Iron .... 0.5 mg
Sodium .... 3 mg
Potassium .... 244 mg
Vitamin A .... 900 IU
Vitamin B1 ..... 0.06 mg
Vitamin B2 ..... 0.04 mg
Vitamin B3 .... 0.7 mg
Vitamin C .... 23 mg
kJ 88
Calories 21

Most people think of the tomato as a vegetable but in fact it is a fruit. The recipes using tomato juice have been included in this section as the tomato is used primarily as a vegetable and in savoury rather than sweet juices. Plump red tomatoes, especially home-grown varieties, will yield the tastiest and greatest quantity of juice and can be juiced alone or combined with most vegetable and many fruit juices.

The organic elements of the tomato neutralise the acid environment of the body. It is a good source of vitamins A, C and E. The juice is said to be beneficial for stimulating blood circulation, liver cleansing and blood purifying and fighting gallstones, gout, rheumatism and even sinus problems.

If you combine tomato juice with a meal containing sugar or starch you will neutralise the alkaline reaction.

Tomato Juice

400 g/14 oz tomatoes

- Wash the tomatoes and cut to fit the juicer.
- Push the tomato through the juicer using the safety plunger.

Tomato juice is best undiluted. See colour plate opposite page 122.

Tomato and Apple Juice

300 g/10½ oz tomatoes
150 g/5 oz apples

- Wash the tomatoes and cut to fit the juicer.
- Wash the apples, remove the cores and cut the fruit to fit the juicer.
- Push the tomato and apple through the juicer using the safety plunger.

Serve this juice over ice with fresh mint.

Tomato and Beetroot Juice

300 g/10½ oz tomatoes
100 g/3½ oz beetroot

- Wash the tomatoes and beetroot and cut to fit the juicer.
- Push the tomato and beetroot through the juicer using the safety plunger.

Add some freshly chopped mint for a great flavour variation.

Tomato, Cucumber and Alfalfa Juice

100 g/3½ oz tomato
150 g/5 oz cucumber
150 g/5 oz alfalfa
  sprouts

- Wash the tomato and cut to fit the juicer.
- Peel the cucumber and cut to fit the juicer.
- Push the alfalfa sprouts, cucumber and tomato through the juicer using the safety plunger.

Tomato Energy Cocktail

100 g/3¹/₂ oz tomatoes
100 g/3¹/₂ oz carrots
50 g/2 oz celery
50 g/2 oz cucumber
50 g/2 oz spinach
50 g/2 oz red capsicum

- Wash the tomatoes and cut to fit the juicer.
- Wash the carrots and cut to fit the juicer.
- Wash the celery. Do not remove the foliage.
- Peel the cucumber and cut to fit the juicer.
- Wash the spinach.
- Wash the capsicum, remove the seeds and cut to fit the juicer.
- Push the tomato and vegetables through the juicer using the safety plunger.

Tomato and Orange Juice

200 g/7 oz tomatoes
200 g/7 oz oranges
small handful of basil

- Wash the tomatoes and cut to fit the juicer.
- Peel the oranges, leaving half the white pith, and cut to fit the juicer.
- Push the tomato, orange and basil through the juicer using the safety plunger.

Watercress

Nutrients per 100 g/3½ oz

Protein	2.2 g
Fat	0.3 g
Carbohydrate	3 g
Calcium	151 mg
Phosphorus	54 mg
Magnesium	20 mg
Iron	1.7 mg
Sodium	52 mg
Potassium	282 mg
Vitamin A	4900 IU
Vitamin B1	0.08 mg
Vitamin B2	0.16 mg
Vitamin B3	0.9 mg
Vitamin C	79 mg
kJ	80
Calories	20

Watercress juice is regarded as a powerful intestinal cleanser and toxin neutraliser. It is good for the kidneys, bladder, blood circulation, reducing inflammation, cleansing skin, and body toning and is a good source of vitamin C, calcium and potassium. Watercress is also high in sulphur, which makes it alkaline-forming, and chlorophyll, which stimulates oxygen metabolism and good circulation and ensures a healthy heart. Watercress stimulates fat burning, so is ideal for people on weight-loss programmes.

Because of the potency of watercress juice it is best to drink small quantities (up to 60 ml/2 fl oz/¼ cup) or to dilute the juice with water or other juices, such as carrot or celery.

Watercress Juice

100 g/3¹/₂ oz watercress

- Wash the watercress thoroughly and shake dry.
- Push the watercress through the juicer using the safety plunger.

Watercress juice can be diluted 1 part juice to 1–4 parts water.

Watercress and Carrot Juice

50 g/2 oz watercress
350 g/12 oz carrots

- Wash the watercress thoroughly and shake dry.
- Wash the carrots and cut to fit the juicer.
- Push the watercress and carrot through the juicer using the safety plunger.

Watercress and Orange Juice

50 g/2 oz watercress
350 g/12 oz oranges

- Wash the watercress thoroughly and shake dry.
- Peel the oranges, leaving half the white pith, and cut to fit the juicer.
- Push the watercress and orange through the juicer using the safety plunger.

Watercress and Vegetable Cocktail

50 g/2 oz watercress
200 g/7 oz carrots
100 g/3¹/₂ oz celery
50 g/2 oz spinach
1 spring onion

- Wash the watercress thoroughly and shake dry.
- Wash the carrots and cut to fit the juicer.
- Wash the celery. Do not remove the foliage.
- Wash the spinach thoroughly and shake dry.
- Wash the spring onion.
- Push the vegetables through the juicer using the safety plunger.

Soups

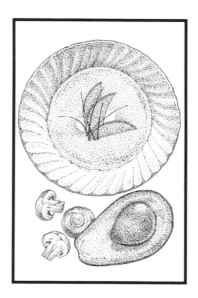

With a juicer you can make delicious chilled soups in just minutes. The recipes that follow are ideal to serve on a hot summer's evening before the main meal or for an easy lunch when partnered by a salad and wholesome crusty bread. When making some of these soups you may need to use a blender (hand-held or otherwise) or food-processor to achieve a smooth texture.

Most of the soups for which I have supplied recipes can be heated gently, but don't forget that as soon as you heat vegetables and fruits you lose much of their nutrient value and destroy the living enzymes within the food.

To make thick and creamy soups simply stir through low-fat yoghurt to achieve the desired consistency. For extra nutrition and fibre, add some grated vegetables to your soups or a handful of lentils or sprouts.

I have also included a recipe for Barley Broth (see page 156), which in fact does not use any juice. However, the strained broth can be added to any of the soups given here to extend them and add extra flavour and nutrition. Barley is an excellent source of protein and its addition will make any soup a complete meal.

Use the following recipes as a guideline and experiment with making soups; keep a note of your successes as you go.

Asparagus, Apple and Avocado Soup

SERVES 2
100 g/3¹/₂ oz asparagus
300 g/10¹/₂ oz apples
2.5 cm/1 inch piece
  ginger, peeled
100 g/3¹/₂ oz avocado
  flesh
freshly ground black
  pepper

- Wash the asparagus.
- Wash the apples, remove the cores and cut the fruit to fit the juicer.
- Push the asparagus, apple and ginger through the juicer using safety plunger.
- Blend the avocado and the juice until smooth.
- Season with black pepper and chill briefly before serving.

Avocado Soup

SERVES 2-3
200 g/7 oz celery
300 g/10¹/₂ oz carrots
150 g/5 oz avocado
  flesh
squeeze of lemon juice
freshly ground black
  pepper
2 tablespoons finely
  chopped fresh chives

- Wash the celery. Do not remove the foliage.
- Wash the carrots and cut to fit the juicer.
- Push the celery and carrots through the juicer using the safety plunger.
- Blend the avocado and juice until smooth. Add the lemon juice and black pepper to taste and chill briefly before serving.
- Garnish with chives.

Cream of Avocado Soup

SERVES 4
400 g/14 oz celery
450 g/1 lb apples
400 g/14 oz avocado
  flesh
125 ml/4 fl oz/1/2 cup
  low-fat yoghurt
freshly ground black
  pepper
2 tablespoons finely
  chopped fresh chives

- Wash the celery. Do not remove the foliage.
- Wash the apples, remove the cores and cut the fruit to fit the juicer.
- Push the celery and apple through the juicer using the safety plunger.
- Blend the avocado and juice until smooth.
- Stir the yoghurt through the juice and season with black pepper.
- Chill briefly and garnish with chives before serving.

See colour plate opposite page 123.

Carrot, Apple and Walnut Soup

SERVES 4
1 kg/2 lb 4 oz carrots
900 g/2 lb apples
1/4 cup/3 tablespoons
  walnuts

- Wash the carrots and cut to fit the juicer.
- Wash the apples, remove the cores and cut the fruit to fit the juicer.
- Push the carrot and apple through the juicer using the safety plunger.
- Chop the walnuts very finely or grind them to a fine powder and stir through the juice. Chill briefly before serving.

Carrot and Herb Soup

SERVES 2–3
1 kg/2 lb 4 oz carrots
200 g/7 oz celery
1/2 cup/6 tablespoons
  finely chopped fresh
  herbs
1/2 teaspoon ground
  cummin

- Wash the carrots and cut to fit the juicer.
- Wash the celery. Do not remove the foliage.
- Push the carrots and celery through the juicer using the safety plunger.
- Stir the fresh herbs and cummin through the juice and chill briefly before serving.

Parsley, chives, thyme, oregano, marjoram and basil all complement this soup.

Carrot and Lemon Soup

SERVES 2–3
1 kg/2 lb 4 oz carrots
200 g/7 oz apples
2 tablespoons lemon juice
1 tablespoon finely grated lemon rind
1 tablespoon chopped fresh thyme or marjoram

- Wash the carrots and cut to fit the juicer.
- Wash the apples, remove the cores and cut the fruit to fit the juicer.
- Push the carrot and apple through the juicer using the safety plunger.
- Stir the lemon juice, lemon rind and herbs through the juice and chill briefly before serving.

Carrot, Tomato and Basil Soup

SERVES 4
1 kg/2 lb 4 oz carrots
800 g/1 lb 12 oz tomatoes
¼ cup/3 tablespoons finely chopped fresh basil
freshly ground black pepper

- Wash the carrots and tomatoes and cut to fit the juicer.
- Push the carrot and tomato through the juicer using the safety plunger.
- Stir the fresh basil through the juice, season with plenty of black pepper and chill briefly before serving.

See colour plate opposite page 123.

Curried Carrot, Asparagus and Avocado Soup

SERVES 2
250 g/9 oz carrots
125 g/4½ oz asparagus
100 g/3½ oz avocado flesh
¼ teaspoon curry powder
¼ teaspoon ground cummin
squeeze of lemon juice

- Wash the carrots and cut to fit the juicer.
- Wash the asparagus.
- Push the carrot and asparagus through the juicer using the safety plunger.
- Blend the avocado and juice until smooth.
- Stir the spices through the juice and add lemon juice to taste.
- Chill briefly before serving.

Cucumber, Avocado and Dill Soup

SERVES 2
350 g/12 oz cucumber
100 g/3½ oz avocado
  flesh
1 tablespoon finely
  chopped fresh dill
freshly ground black
  pepper

- Peel the cucumber and cut to fit the juicer.
- Push the cucumber through the juicer using the safety plunger.
- Blend the avocado and juice until smooth.
- Stir the fresh dill through the juice and season with black pepper.
- Chill briefly before serving.

Gazpacho

SERVES 4–6
1 kg/2 lb 4 oz tomatoes
200 g/7 oz carrots
150 g/5 oz cucumber
2 cloves garlic, peeled
2 tablespoons finely
  chopped fresh herbs
freshly ground black
  pepper

- Wash the tomatoes and carrots and cut to fit the juicer.
- Peel the cucumber and cut to fit the juicer.
- Push the tomato, carrot, cucumber and garlic through the juicer using the safety plunger.
- Stir the fresh herbs through the juice, season with plenty of black pepper and chill briefly before serving.

Basil, oregano and thyme can all be used to flavour this soup.

Green Soup

SERVES 2
200 g/7 oz watercress
200 g/7 oz cucumber
100 g/3½ oz avocado
  flesh
1 tablespoon finely
  chopped fresh basil
1 tablespoon finely
  chopped fresh mint

- Wash the watercress.
- Peel the cucumber and cut to fit the juicer.
- Push the watercress and cucumber through the juicer using the safety plunger.
- Blend the avocado and juice until smooth.
- Stir the fresh herbs through the juice and chill briefly before serving.

Melon Soup

SERVES 2
200 g/ 7 oz cantaloup
200 g/ 7 oz honeydew
  melon
2.5 cm/1 inch piece
  ginger, peeled
1 tablespoon finely
  chopped fresh mint

- Peel the cantaloup and honeydew melon, remove the seeds and cut to fit the juicer.
- Push the melon and ginger through the juicer using the safety plunger.
- Stir the fresh mint through the juice and chill briefly before serving.

Cream of Tomato and Basil Soup

SERVES 4 – 6
1 kg/ 2 lb 4 oz tomatoes
200 g/ 7 oz carrots
150 g/5 oz cucumber
100 g/3¹/₂ oz red
  capsicum
250 ml/8 fl oz/1 cup
  low-fat yoghurt
2 tablespoons finely
  chopped fresh basil

- Wash the tomatoes and carrots and cut to fit the juicer.
- Peel the cucumber and cut to fit the juicer.
- Wash the capsicum, remove the seeds and cut to fit the juicer.
- Push the tomato, carrot, cucumber and capsicum through the juicer using the safety plunger.
- Stir the yoghurt and fresh basil through the juice and chill briefly before serving.

Watermelon and Chive Soup

SERVES 2 – 4
600 g/1 lb 5 oz
  watermelon flesh
2 tablespoons finely
  chopped fresh chives
freshly ground black
  pepper

- Cut the watermelon to fit the juicer.
- Push the watermelon through the juicer using the safety plunger.
- Stir the chives through the juice and season with black pepper.
- Chill briefly before serving

Watermelon Gazpacho

SERVES 2
300 g/10¹/₂ oz
  watermelon flesh
250 g/9 oz cucumber
400 g/14 oz tomatoes
1–2 cloves garlic,
  peeled
2 spring onions, finely
  sliced
1 tablespoon finely
  chopped fresh basil

- Cut the watermelon to fit the juicer.
- Peel the cucumber and cut to fit the juicer.
- Wash the tomatoes and cut to fit the juicer.
- Push the watermelon, cucumber, tomato and garlic through the juicer using the safety plunger.
- Stir the spring onions and basil through the juice and chill briefly before serving.

Barley Broth

100 g/3¹/₂ oz carrot
100 g/3¹/₂ oz pumpkin
100 g/3¹/₂ oz parsnip
200 g/7 oz onion
100 g/3¹/₂ oz potato
200 g/7 oz celery
1 cup/1¹/₂ oz roughly
  chopped parsley
3.5 litres/6 pints/
  3³/₄ quarts water
³/₄ cup/5 oz barley
freshly ground black
  pepper

- Grate the carrot, pumpkin and parsnip.
- Dice the onion and cube the potato.
- Slice the celery finely.
- Put all the ingredients in a large stock pot and bring them to the boil.
- Simmer for 2 hours.

Add a little strained broth to any of the soups included here. I like to use the remaining vegetables in a filling for pasties.

Smoothies

Smoothies are thick, luscious drinks usually made from fresh juices, milk and yoghurt. In the following recipes I have substituted bananas for the milk and yoghurt to get the same smooth, creamy consistency. Not only do bananas add a great taste to these smoothies but they are also a complete protein in themselves as they contain all eight of the essential amino acids. Their natural sugar and fibre make them a high-energy food too. This makes a smoothie an easy, nourishing meal substitute. It's hard to believe that anything that tastes this good could be so healthy for you!

To break down the sugar in smoothies you can dilute them by adding low-fat milk, low-fat soy milk or almond milk (see the recipe on page 158). By using any of these liquids you are adding a protein value and improving the nutritional value of the food.

You can also add bran for extra fibre or sesame seeds and lecithin for extra protein and essential unsaturated fatty acids. These will all add a distinctive nutty flavour to a smoothie.

You will need to use a blender (hand-held or otherwise) as well as a juicer when making smoothies. Each of the following recipes serves one.

Almond Milk

Almond milk is a delicious high-calcium alternative to cow's milk. It is ideal for anyone who has an allergy to dairy foods and it is very easily digested. The almonds provide an easily assimilated source of calcium and contain essential unsaturated fatty acids. Almond milk adds protein to these, which are otherwise rich in nutrients and high in energy.

20 almonds
250 ml/8 fl oz/1 cup cold water
vanilla essence to taste

- In a small bowl, pour boiling water over the almonds and leave to stand for a few minutes.
- Pour off the hot water, rub off the almond skins and process the nuts until very fine.
- Slowly add the cold water and process until you have a rich and creamy milk.
- Add vanilla to taste.
- Keep the almond milk refrigerated.

Apple Passion

450 g/1 lb apples
2 passionfruit
100 g/3½ oz banana

- Wash the apples, remove the cores and cut the fruit to fit the juicer.
- Push the apple through the juicer using the safety plunger.
- Cut the passionfruit in half and scoop out the juice and pulp.
- Peel and chop the banana.
- Blend the banana, passionfruit and juice to a creamy consistency.

Blueberry Angel

100 g/3¹/₂ oz blueberries
300 g/10¹/₂ oz oranges
100 g/3¹/₂ oz banana

- Wash the blueberries.
- Peel the oranges, leaving half the white pith, and cut to fit the juicer.
- Push the blueberries and orange through the juicer using the safety plunger.
- Peel and chop the banana.
- Blend the banana and juice to a creamy consistency.

Cantaloup Bliss

350 g/12 oz cantaloup
100 g/3¹/₂ oz banana

- Peel the cantaloup, remove the seeds and cut to fit the juicer.
- Push the cantaloup through the juicer using the safety plunger.
- Peel and chop the banana.
- Blend the banana and juice to a creamy consistency.

Jamaican Dream

200 g/7 oz pineapple
*   flesh*
100 g/3¹/₂ oz banana
125 ml/4 fl oz/¹/₂ cup
*   fresh coconut milk*
2 tablespoons grated
*   fresh coconut*

- Cut the pineapple to fit the juicer.
- Push the pineapple through the juicer using the safety plunger.
- Peel and chop the banana.
- Blend the banana, juice, coconut milk and grated coconut to a creamy consistency.

See colour plate opposite page 138.

Pear Delight

250 g/9 oz pears
200 g/7 oz apples
100 g/3¹/₂ oz banana
nutmeg to taste

- Wash the pears and apples, remove the cores and cut the fruit to fit juicer.
- Push the pear and apple through the juicer using the safety plunger.
- Peel and chop the banana.
- Blend the banana and juice to a creamy consistency.
- Add nutmeg to taste.

Pineapple-ana

200 g/7 oz pineapple
* flesh*
200 g/7 oz apples
100 g/3¹/₂ oz banana

- Cut the pineapple to fit the juicer.
- Wash the apples, remove the cores and cut the fruit to fit the juicer.
- Push the pineapple and apple through the juicer using the safety plunger.
- Peel and chop the banana.
- Blend the banana and juice to a creamy consistency.

Pink Lady

100 g/3¹/₂ oz
* raspberries*
300 g/10¹/₂ oz apples
100 g/3¹/₂ oz banana

- Wash the raspberries.
- Wash the apples, remove the cores and cut the fruit to fit the juicer.
- Push the raspberries and apple through the juicer using the safety plunger.
- Peel and chop the banana.
- Blend the banana and juice to a creamy consistency.

Summer Bliss

150 g/5 oz mango flesh
350 g/12 oz
  strawberries
100 g/3¹/₂ oz bananas

- Cut the mango to fit the juicer.
- Wash and hull the strawberries.
- Push the mango and strawberries through the juicer using the safety plunger.
- Peel and chop the banana.
- Blend the banana and juice to a creamy consistency.

See colour plate opposite page 138.

Sunshine Sizzler

150 g/5 oz mango flesh
100 g/3¹/₂ oz pineapple
  flesh
2 passionfruit
100 g/3¹/₂ oz banana
125 ml/4 fl oz/¹/₂ cup
  fresh coconut milk
1 tablespoon grated
  fresh coconut

- Cut the mango and pineapple to fit the juicer.
- Push the mango and pineapple through the juicer using the safety plunger.
- Cut the passionfruit in half and scoop out the juice and pulp.
- Peel and chop the banana.
- Blend the banana, juice, coconut milk and grated coconut to a creamy consistency.

Tropical Blush

100 g/3¹/₂ oz apricots
250 g/9 oz nectarines
200 g/7 oz oranges
100 g/3¹/₂ oz banana

- Wash the apricots and nectarines, remove the stones and cut to fit the juicer.
- Peel the oranges, leaving half the white pith, and cut to fit the juicer.
- Push the apricot, nectarine and orange through the juicer using the safety plunger.
- Peel and chop the banana.
- Blend the banana and juice to a creamy consistency.

Island Breeze

200 g/ 7 oz papaw
200 g/ 7 oz oranges
100 g/3¹/₂ oz banana
60 ml/ 2 fl oz/¹/₄ cup
fresh coconut milk
2 tablespoons grated
fresh coconut

- Peel the papaw, remove the seeds and cut to fit the juicer.
- Peel the oranges, leaving half the white pith, and cut to fit the juicer.
- Push the papaw and orange through the juicer using the safety plunger.
- Peel and chop the banana.
- Blend the banana, juice, coconut milk and grated coconut to a creamy consistency.

Sorbets

Sorbets are delicious frozen desserts made from fresh juices. If you are fortunate enough to own an ice-cream maker you can simply add your fresh juice sweetened with syrup water (see recipes below) and let the machine do all the work for you. Otherwise, you can pour the sorbet mixture into a metal dish and freeze it. Do not allow it to freeze rock hard or you won't be able to scoop it out. Should your sorbet set hard you can process it back to an icy consistency with the help of a food processor.

Syrup Water 1

Collect the fibre left over when juicing citrus and other sweet fruit and cover it with water (1 part fibre to 7 parts water) in a saucepan. (Do not add sour fruit fibre as it will give the syrup a very tart flavour.) Bring the mixture to the boil and simmer until reduced by a quarter. Strain the liquid and store it in the refrigerator. Use the syrup water to sweeten your sorbets.

Syrup Water 2

Combine 60 ml/2 fl oz/¼ cup apple juice concentrate and 250 ml/8 fl oz/ 1 cup water and mix well. Store in the refrigerator and use to sweeten your sorbets.

Apple juice concentrate can be purchased at most health-food shops or in the frozen-food section in some supermarkets. Dilute it to suit your own tastes.

Berry Fantasy Sorbet

SERVES 4
400 g/14 oz blueberries
200 g/7 oz raspberries
750 g/1 lb 10 oz
  strawberries
250 ml/8 fl oz/1 cup
  syrup water

- Wash the berries and hull the strawberries.
- Push the berries through the juicer using the safety plunger.
- Add ¼ cup/3 tablespoons berry fibre to the juice with the syrup water and mix together.
- Pour the mixture into a metal tray and freeze or use an ice-cream maker.

Serve with fresh berries and rose petals.

Kiwi Islander Sorbet

SERVES 4
1.5 kg/3 lb 8 oz kiwifruit
450 g/1 lb apples or
  pears
1 passionfruit
250 ml/8 fl oz/1 cup
  syrup water

- Peel the furry skin from the kiwifruit and cut the fruit to fit the juicer.
- Wash the apples or pears, remove the cores and cut the fruit to fit the juicer.
- Push the kiwifruit and apple or pear through the juicer using the safety plunger.
- Cut the passionfruit in half and scoop out the juice and pulp.
- Combine the fruit juice, passionfruit juice and pulp and syrup water and mix well.
- Pour the mixture into a metal tray and freeze or use an ice-cream maker.

See colour plate opposite page 139.

Lemon and Pear Sorbet

SERVES 4
150 g/5 oz lemon
1.5 kg/3 lb 8 oz pears
1 tablespoon finely
  grated lemon rind
1 tablespoon finely
  grated orange rind
250 ml/8 fl oz/1 cup
  syrup water

- Peel the lemons and cut to fit the juicer.
- Wash the pears, remove the cores and cut the fruit to fit the juicer.
- Push the lemon and pear through the juicer using the safety plunger.
- Combine the juice, rinds and syrup water and mix well.
- Pour the mixture into a metal tray and freeze or use an ice-cream maker.

Serve with strawberries and kiwifruit.

Mango and Banana Sorbet

SERVES 4

1 kg/ 2 lb 4 oz mango flesh
200 g/ 7 oz bananas
squeeze of lemon juice
250 ml/8 fl oz/1 cup syrup water

You will need to use a blender (hand-held or otherwise) in this recipe.

• Cut the mango flesh to fit the juicer.
• Push the mango through the juicer using the safety plunger.
• Peel and chop the bananas.
• Blend the banana, mango juice and lemon juice until thick and creamy.
• Add the syrup water to the fruit mixture and stir through.
• Pour the mixture into a metal tray and freeze or use an ice-cream maker.

Serve with a selection of tropical fruits.

Orange and Passionfruit Sorbet

SERVES 4
1.25 kg/ 2 lb 13 oz oranges
6 passionfruit
250 ml/8 fl oz/1 cup syrup water

• Peel the oranges, leaving half the white pith, and cut to fit the juicer.
• Push the oranges through the juicer using the safety plunger.
• Cut the passionfruit in halves and scoop out the juice and pulp.
• Combine the orange juice, passionfruit juice and pulp and the syrup water.
• Pour the mixture into a metal tray and freeze or use an ice-cream maker.

Serve with orange slices, banana and pineapple chunks and sprigs of fresh mint. See colour plate opposite page 139.

Pineapple Tang

SERVES 4
800 g/1 lb 12 oz
    pineapple flesh
450 g/1 lb apples
squeeze of lemon juice
250 ml/8 fl oz/1 cup
    syrup water

- Cut the pineapple to fit the juicer.
- Wash the apples, remove the cores and cut the fruit to fit the juicer.
- Push the pineapple and apple through juicer using the safety plunger.
- Combine the pineapple and apple juice with the lemon juice and syrup water and mix well.
- Pour the mixture into a metal tray and freeze or use an ice-cream maker.

Herbs and Spices for Juicing

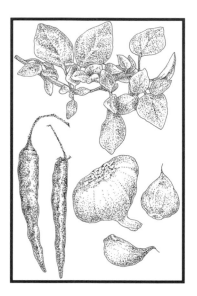

Basil

This herb has distinctive, bright-green flat leaves with pointed tips and a sweet, spicy and somewhat clove-like flavour. It complements tomato juice perfectly and is also excellent for adding to any vegetable soups.

Caraway

The herb has frond-like leaves and the seeds, which are rich in aromatic oils, are used as a spice. Caraway is prized for its aid to digestion. It can be added to tomato, carrot, apple, pear or vegetable juices.

Cayenne Pepper

This spice, a dull-red powder made from members of the chilli pepper family, is hot to taste. It is said to be good for digestion and acts as an appetite stimulant. It can be added to tomato, carrot and green juices to add a warm bite.

Chilli

Available fresh, dried, powdered or as seeds only, chillies, used sparingly, can add punch to your vegetable juices like no other spice. These fiery small members of the pepper family are high in vitamin C and are said to aid slimming.

Chives

Chives, a herb, belong to the onion family but do not have the typical onion-like bulb. The mild onion flavour is found in their grass-like stems. They are considered an appetite stimulant, good for digestion and helpful for anaemia. Chives are excellent for adding to all soup recipes.

Cinnamon

Cinnamon, from the bark of a tree native to Sri Lanka, comes as a fine brownish powder or in rolled-up quill form. It has a sweet aromatic flavour and is a popular addition to apple, pear, peach and melon juice. Medicinally this spice is used in many preparations to stimulate the appetite, treat nausea and cramps, as a sedative and in dental procedures to deaden the nerves.

Coriander

The herb coriander has lacy, feathery foliage and a spicy, aromatic flavour. The ground seeds are also used in cooking. Fresh coriander can be juiced along with other vegetables, while the ground seeds can be stirred through a vegetable juice as a quick-and-easy flavour enhancer.

Dill

The dark-green feather-like foliage of the herb dill has a dry aromatic flavour like aniseed. The dried seeds are used as a spice. Dill is said to help an upset stomach, relieve hiccups, help insomnia and sweeten one's breath. Try it in apple, pear, celery carrot and cucumber juices. It is also delicious in soups.

Fennel

Fresh fennel, which has flesh like that of celery and aromatic foliage similar to dill, can be added to vegetable juice for a slightly aniseed taste. Nutritionally this herb is similar to celery and is rich in alkaline minerals. However, it is lower in sodium and higher in energy-producing natural sugars. With high levels of calcium and magnesium it is considered helpful in relaxing and calming nerves. Add a little fennel to a vegetable juice just before going to bed to stimulate a good night's sleep.

Garlic

Garlic was known to the Chinese in 2000 BC and has been used medicinally there ever since for a wide variety of ailments and as a health restorer. It continues today to be used for the treatment of colds, influenza, bronchitis, asthma, infection, cancer, heart disease, high blood pressure, diarrhoea and even as an aphrodisiac. It is also said to be one of nature's most effective antibiotics. Garlic is a bulbous plant that comes from the onion family and has a pungent flavour. It can be added to almost all vegetable juices and soups.

Ginger

When peeled the gnarly ginger root or rhizome is woody and fibrous yet moist and yields a delicate, piquant flavour. Ginger can also be used in its dried powder form but fresh ginger is always used in the recipes in this book. This spice can be added to all vegetable and fruit juices and is particularly good in carrot, apple, melon, grape or strawberry juice.

Kelp

Kelp is not, in fact, a herb or spice: it is a type of seaweed. However, it is worth mentioning here because it can be added to vegetable juices or soups as a salt substitute. It is highly nutritious with perfect mineral balance (it is particularly high in iodine). Kelp is said to be helpful for obesity because it stimulates the thyroid gland to increase the metabolic rate.

Marjoram

The most common form of the herb marjoram is favoured for its aromatic leaves, which are used widely in cooking. The oil from this spicy, slightly pungent herb is said to be good for relieving rheumatic pains, indigestion, toothache and headaches and stimulating sleep. It also has antiseptic qualities. Try marjoram in all vegetable juices and apple, pear or pineapple juice.

Mint

There are a number of different varieties of mint, one of the most common herbs, and the flavour of each is clean and refreshing. Mint is delicious added to apple, pear, strawberry, melon, cucumber, carrot or pineapple juices.

Nutmeg

Nutmeg is an aromatic spice that is available whole as a nut, which is grated, or ground. Nutmeg can be used for flatulence, nausea, vomiting and to improve digestion. It can also be added to drinks last thing at night to stimulate good sleep. Nutmeg complements apple and pear juice particularly well and is also a tasty addition to drinks containing bananas.

Oregano

The herb oregano is very similar in appearance to marjoram (it is actually the wild form of marjoram) but it has a more pungent flavour. It provides the same benefits as marjoram, and should be used in the same way (see Marjoram, above).

Paprika

The spice paprika is the ground seed of the capsicum. A deep reddish colour, its flavour ranges from mild to sweet to mildly hot, making it an ideal accompaniment to vegetable juices.

Parsley

Parsley, probably the most common herb used in cooking today, comes from the carrot family. Its dark-green foliage yields a juice high in chlorophyll, vitamins (especially A and C) and minerals such as calcium, magnesium, phosphorus, potassium, sodium and sulphur. It is highly regarded as a blood toner and body cleanser. The chlorophyll stimulates oxygen metabolism as well as cell respiration and regeneration (parsley is highly regarded in the treatment of cancer). Parsley makes a very concentrated green juice that can be added to most other vegetable juices to increase the nutrient value and enhance the flavour. Because of its potency you should not drink more than 20 ml/1 tablespoon parsley juice at a time. Dilute it with water or other juices, such as celery, carrot, cucumber or apple.

Rosemary

Rosemary is a pungent, highly aromatic herb with dark-green, fine leathery leaves. It should be used in moderation as it can dominate the flavour of other ingredients. Try just a little rosemary in apple, cucumber, carrot and tomato juices. It is said to be good for easing headaches, improving blood circulation and stimulating the senses.

Sage

Of the different varieties of sage, pineapple sage is the most popular to use in drinks. This herb is said to aid digestion (especially of rich and fatty foods) and help soothe sore throats. Pineapple sage has also been used to treat coughs, colds, headaches and fever. It is ideal with green juices, beetroot juice and apple or pineapple juice.

Thyme

The many varieties of thyme have sweet, aromatic dark-green or variegated tiny leaves. It has been used for aches and pains (especially associated with menstruation), sore throats, laryngitis, bronchitis and whooping cough. Thyme is especially popular as a mouth deodoriser. Use this herb in vegetable juices and apple, pear or pineapple juices.

Glossary

Although some of the language and spellings in this book may be unfamiliar to the American home cook, most of the information is straightforward and easy to decipher. But to help you get the most from the recipes and information, we have assembled a short glossary of ingredients and terms.

acerola berries: small, cherry-like fruit also called Barbados cherries.

beetroot: beets.

biscuits: cookies.

capsicum, red, green and yellow: bell peppers.

jam doughnut: jelly doughnut.

kilojoules: an amount of food having an energy-producing value such as a calorie. There are approximately four calories in one kilojoule.

lemon cordial: citrus-flavoured soft drink.

pawpaw: papaya.

pips: seeds.

potato crisp: potato chip.

silverbeet: dark green leafy vegetable, similar to spinach.

sweet cream biscuits: cream-filled cookies.

Index